COURAGE AND COMPASSION

Courage and Compassion

*A Jewish Boyhood in
German-Occupied Greece*

Tony Molho

berghahn
NEW YORK • OXFORD
www.berghahnbooks.com

Published in 2024 by
Berghahn Books
www.berghahnbooks.com

English-language edition
© 2024 Tony Molho

Greek-language edition
© 2022 Patakis Editions & Αντώνης Μόλχο

Originally published in Greek as
Η Κοινοτοπία του Καλού. Ένα εβραιόπουλο στην Ελλάδα της Κατοχής

All rights reserved. Except for the quotation of short passages
for the purposes of criticism and review, no part of this book
may be reproduced in any form or by any means, electronic or
mechanical, including photocopying, recording, or any information
storage and retrieval system now known or to be invented,
without written permission of the publisher.

Library of Congress Cataloging-in-Publication Data
Names: Molho, Anthony, author.
Title: Courage and compassion : a Jewish boyhood in German-occupied Greece / Tony Molho.
Other titles: Hē koinotopia tou kalou. English. | Jewish boyhood in German-occupied Greece
Description: English-language edition. | New York : Berghahn Books, 2024. | "Originally published in Greek as H Koinotopia toy Kaloú. Ena evraiópoylo sthn Ellada thς Katochης."
Identifiers: LCCN 2024009948 (print) | LCCN 2024009949 (ebook) | ISBN 9781805394839 (hardback) | ISBN 9781805394846 (paperback) | ISBN 9781805394853 (epub)
Subjects: LCSH: Molho, Anthony—Childhood and youth. | Hidden children (Holocaust)—Greece—Biography. | Jews—Greece—Thessalonikē—History—20th century. | Jewish children—Greece—Thessalonikē. | Jewish children in the Holocaust—Greece—Thessalonikē—Personal narratives. | Holocaust, Jewish (1939–1945)—Greece—Personal narratives. | Greece—History—Occupation, 1941–1944. | Thessalonikē (Greece)—Biography.
Classification: LCC D804.48 .M65 2024 (print) | LCC D804.48 (ebook) | DDC 940.53/18092 [B]—dc23/eng/20240229
LC record available at https://lccn.loc.gov/2024009948
LC ebook record available at https://lccn.loc.gov/2024009949

British Library Cataloguing in Publication Data
A catalogue record for this book is available from the British Library

ISBN 978-1-80539-483-9 hardback
ISBN 978-1-80539-484-6 paperback
ISBN 978-1-80539-485-3 epub
ISBN 978-1-80539-486-0 web pdf

https://doi.org/10.3167/9781805394839

That's the core. The early part of you.[1]

These things cannot be written. Human beings cannot write these things.[2]

Il n'est plus question de distinctions superficielles de race, de religion, ni de rang social—je n'y ai jamais cru—il y a l'union contre le mal, et la communion contre la souffrance.[3]

---

[1] Kirk Douglas, *The New York Times*, 6 February 2020, "Obituary of Kirk Douglas."
[2] Lily Alkalay Molho in 1993, conversation recorded in video by Mr. Izo Avram.
[3] Hélène Berr, *Journal*, Paris, Tallandier, 2008, pp. 107–108. Entry dated 18 July 1942.

Contents

List of Illustrations   viii

Foreword   xii
    Katherine E. Fleming

Chapter 1. Memory's Reach   1

Chapter 2. Being Greek   17

Chapter 3. Hide and Seek   50

Chapter 4. *Fuga* or the Long March   73

Chapter 5. Soeur Hélène   95

Chapter 6. In the Labyrinth   121

Chapter 7. A Yearning for Home   144

Chapter 8. A City of Ghosts   166

Chapter 9. *Incipit Vita Nuova*   185

Chapter 10. After the End   217

Postscript   227

Acknowledgments   231

Illustrations

Figure 1.1 (a) My maternal grandfather Nissim Alkalay, and (b) My maternal grandmother Henrietta Alkalay. Both were murdered in Auschwitz. The pictures were taken at the end of the 1920s or beginning of the 1930s.   2

Figure 2.1. Uncle Richard, my mother's brother, in the mid-1920s. He was murdered in Auschwitz.   19

Figure 2.2. The street gang on Evzonon Street. I took this photograph myself sometime in the early 1950s with a camera given me as a present by Uncle Mousa. My sister, Marcella, who had been born in 1946, is sitting in the middle of the front row.   26

Figure 2.3. My parents' wedding picture, May 1937. Liolia Christidou, our neighbor, sits in front of the newlyweds.   33

Figure 2.4. My mother's graduation picture from Anatolia College, 1934. She stands fourth from right.   34

Figure 2.5. My parents at the time of their engagement, February 1937.   35

Figure 2.6. Marriage contract for my parents' wedding, December 1936. It was written in Ladino, in *solitreo* script.   36

ILLUSTRATIONS

Figure 2.7. (a) My maternal great-grandmother, and also (b) My maternal great-grandfather. I do not know their names. Both pictures were probably taken in the early years of the twentieth century. 38

Figure 2.8. (a) My paternal grandfather, Lazar Molho, son of Saul, and (b) My paternal grandmother Flora Hasson. Both pictures were taken in the 1920s or 1930s. 39

Figure 2.9. The Alkalay family. The photograph was taken in 1917 or 1918, in the Antonio Porcessi Studio. My grandfather Nissim stands, my grandmother Henrietta, wearing the half traditional dress, sits, my Uncle Richard and my mother stand. 41

Figure 2.10. The author, about two years old, not at all ready for the adventures that awaited him. 43

Figure 2.11. With my mother, autumn/winter 1940, in the White Tower Gardens. 45

Figure 3.1. My mother, standing in front row, the last one on the right, with her classmates at the Lycée Français, 1919–20. 64

Figure 3.2. My father's graduation, perhaps in 1916, from the (French?) school. My father, standing, last on the right. His brother, my Uncle Isaac, sitting, second from left. 65

Figure 3.3. Aunt Marcella, my mother's younger sister. Murdered in Auschwitz. Photo perhaps taken at the time of her engagement to Pepo Carasso, early 1940s. 65

ILLUSTRATIONS

Figure 4.1. (a) Three immediate postwar documents. My mother's Red Cross ID, 1945. (b) My father's police ID card, 2 July 1945, with his religion listed as "Mosaic." (c) My mother's police ID, 19 January 1946.   89

Figure 5.1. Two pictures, both taken in 1956, shortly before our departure for the United States: (a) My father, (b) My mother.   107

Figure 9.1. Alberto Molho, 1904–1945, known as Napolitan, journalist, author of theatrical works, and one of my father's five younger brothers.   188

Figure 9.2. School excursion. I am sitting second from right. Sitting wearing a baseball cap, our American teacher Mr. Yoder (But I am unsure if this was his name!), 1955–1956.   193

Figure 9.3. Bazaar at Anatolia College, I stand fifth from left, 1955.   197

Figure 9.4. With my mother and sister Marcella, born on 3 July 1946. The photograph was taken in the autumn of 1946.   200

Figure 9.5. Wedding photograph of Uncle Raphael (Roufa) and Aunt Henrietta, 1947; she had returned from Auschwitz about two years earlier.   202

Figure 9.6. With my sister, Marcella, at Uncle Isaac and aunt Rita's wedding, 1949.   205

Figure 9.7. Uncle Isaac's and aunt Rita's wedding in 1949, with my sister Marcella, aged three, as flower girl.   207

ILLUSTRATIONS

Figure 9.8. My mother on the day she received her doctorate (Ph.D.) degree at Western Reserve University in Cleveland, Ohio, 1965.   212

Figure 9.9. My police ID, 1955.   214

Figure 9.10. At Brown University, summer 1966.   215

Figure 9.11. With my mother, a few weeks before her death in August 2006.   216

Foreword

> April is the cruelest month, breeding
> Lilacs out of the dead land, mixing
> Memory and desire, stirring
> Dull roots with spring rain.
> Winter kept us warm, covering
> Earth in forgetful snow, feeding
> A little life with dried tubers.
> —T. S. Eliot, "The Wasteland"

In mid-April of 1945, young Tony Molho returned at last to his home in Salonica after two years in hiding—or more precisely, of being hidden—from Greece's Nazi occupiers. He was not yet six years old. The day was sunny, and he could feel around him the excitement of homecoming. As he stepped into the back garden, the sight of a glorious wisteria blooming against the garden wall further buoyed his spirits.

This scene comes close to the end of this memoir, and one might think it is an ending to Molho's tale. And while the image of spring rebirth might seem an unqualifiedly happy one, the reality (as it usually is) was more complex. Molho writes, "what happened after our return home is another story." On one level, of course, he means: This memoir is about the war; it would take another to tell the story of my life after it. Yet there is a poignant, ultimate irony to the statement, for the deeply moving nature of this memoir derives from its emphatic demonstration that, for Tony (as perhaps indeed for all survivors of the Shoah), there was and has been no "other story." Far from the "before" and "after" being different tales, far from the "after" being "another story," this beautiful memoir shows us the powerful ways our childhood core is what we carry with us over the arc of a lifetime.

And how much more so for those who had a childhood such as his. As Molho writes: "nearly everything important that my parents, sister, and I did after the war was an attempt to reconcile ourselves to the memory of the Shoah and to try, mostly unsuccessfully it turns out, to normalize its influence on our lives. There was no return . . . just the slow unfolding of the war's consequences, which lasted for decades, until my parents' death and my own slow decline."

Tony Molho's memoir, which you are about to have the pleasure of reading, is about many different things. Fundamentally, of course, it is, as its subtitle has it, about "A Jewish Boyhood in German-Occupied Greece." And indeed, it tells us with remarkable forthrightness of just that: the adventures and misadventures of the author's young self, as he was passed quite literally from hand to hand, home to home, in the desperate and ultimately successful bid to save him from death at the hands of the German Nazis who occupied Greece during World War II. It recounts the fierce love and resilience of his parents, who contrived against all odds to keep their young son alive. This small volume, then, tells an immense and dramatic tale, a story of survival under the harshest and most unrelenting of circumstances.

As an account of the incredible events of two early years in Molho's remarkable life, this volume would, as a historical document alone, be an important work. But it is far more than that. Ultimately, it is a meditation on the most profound questions that trouble us all in our moments of reflectiveness: What is the nature of the passage of time? How can it be said that we have a single persisting, intact self that we carry with us from childhood to old age? How does memory draw on multiple threads to weave a coherent story of our lives? And, what is the point of it all? *Is* there a point? It is Molho's musing upon such questions and his tremendous capacity for deep self-reflection even as his dramatic narrative unfolds that makes this volume so much more than "just" a memoir.

No doubt the source of this depth lies, at least in part, in the fact that Molho himself is in turn much more than "just" a memoirist. He is a historian by profession, and a most distinguished one, a world-class scholar of late-medieval Florence. Molho has thought long and hard about the meaning of history, the nature of memory, and the ways remembered pasts echo in and even constitute our present. It may not be too much of a leap to venture that his chosen specialty—the Renaissance—has given him occasion to think long and hard about how we periodicize our histories, attempting to pin them down with artificially imposed "eras" to make them more coherent and compartmentalized. It will also have given him ample time to ponder the ironies of the idea of historical "rebirth." As Molho's wisteria shows us, no less forcefully than Eliot's lilacs, it is in fact at the moment of regeneration—the beginning of "the after"—that we find just how complex it is to attempt a renaissance, to emerge from the forgetful snow of winter and to aspire to a future that is wholly new. It shows us, indeed, how the dead and the living constantly mix together, how life is inevitably nourished by the "dry tubers" of the past.

FOREWORD

While Molho's core narrative ends in 1945, the brilliance of his memoir is that it is suffused with this strange accordioning of time, the never-endingness of what he lived through in those two terrifying years from spring of 1943 until the spring of 1945. Molho allows us to see him—the him of today—in conversation with his young self and indeed reveals that it is this ongoing conversation that has made up perhaps the most meaningful consistent narrative of his life. This volume is striking for its palimpsestic nature, the ease with which it moves back and forth through time, with that "after" serving as a lens onto what came before, just as the dramatic events of those two years have served as constant filter for Molho's whole life. In what way, it asks us, are our pasts ever behind us, and in what ways are they inevitably, always, part of us?

Courage and Compassion is about other things, as well. The nature of good—which, in insightfully reworking Hannah Arendt's famous phrase, Molho describes as being every bit as "banal" as evil—is a restrained yet steady theme. So, too, are important historical questions, Molho's treatment of which will be thought-provoking to historians of twentieth-century Greece: to what extent did—could—Jews think of themselves as Greek? To what extent did Greek Orthodox Christians aid and abet their Nazi occupiers as they went about the dastardly plan to rid Greece of its Jews? (The haunting image of yellow curtains, made of fabric stolen from Molho's family and hanging in the home of Greek Orthodox "friends" after the war, will stay with you long after you have finished reading.) How is it that a whole city managed, virtually overnight, to erase the memory of tens of thousands of its recent inhabitants, to turn them into specters? In a moniker coined by T. S. Eliot for another postwar European city, Salonica had become a "City of Ghosts"—the ep-

FOREWORD

ithet that Molho's mother, Lily, also gave it in an interview some fifty years after the core events described in her son's book. The Shoah did, indeed, render Salonica—one of Europe's most important Jewish metropoles and arguably its most cosmopolitan—a ghostly city, stalked by the phantasms of its recent past. They are ghosts that endure to this day. Books like this one help to bring them out of their shadows, and remind us that the past is not "another story" or a buried winter. Beneath Eliot's "forgetful snow" lie lives and lifetimes that are knitted to ours.

Molho writes, again borrowing a turn of phrase from Eliot, that he feels that he has had "a discontinuous life." In one sense, this memoir suggests that he has: wandering from place to place, from one language to another, from one country to another, from one historical era to the next. But at the end, through his deeply affecting account, I cannot help but feel that, perhaps, he has had a life of remarkable continuity and integration, a lifetime of bravely reckoning with the events recounted in this volume, and sustained by the remarkable love of the parents who worked so hard to save him. The blossoming of lilacs and wisteria is painful, but they are beautiful, after all.

Katherine E. Fleming

1.
Memory's Reach

Sephardi Salonica. That's the universe in which I was born and spent the first few years of my life. My immediate ancestors had lived in this city for several generations. There, they were engaged in commerce—some of them modest and middling merchants and middlemen, such as shipping agents, insurance brokers, money changers and the like, while others were rabbis, and a very few, notably my maternal grandfather, were successful businessmen, cosmopolitan in outlook and familiar with life in Europe's more "advanced" regions. A constant if often muted presence in the stories of their lives—a ghost that casts its shadow on much of what I recount here—is the fact that, starting in 1430 and for almost five centuries, Salonica (Selanik in Turkish, Solun in Bulgarian, Thessaloniki in Greek, Salonique or Thessalonique in French, Salonicco in Italian) was an important commercial and administrative center of the Ottoman Empire and home of the largest Sephardic community in the Balkans and one of the largest in Europe. For long stretches of time since the beginning of the sixteenth century when they had fled the Inquisitions of the Spanish and Portuguese Kingdoms and, on the Sultan's invitation, settled in Salonica, the city's Jews had comprised the majority of its population. There,

Figure 1.1. *(a) My maternal grandfather Nissim Alkalay, and (b) My maternal grandmother Henrietta Alkalay. Both were murdered in Auschwitz. The pictures were taken at the end of the 1920s or beginning of the 1930s.*[1]

they flourished and contributed to Salonica's fame as the New Jerusalem.

Then, in 1912, during the Balkan wars between the Ottoman Empire and the Christian nations of Serbia, Bulgaria, Montenegro, and Greece, Greek armies conquered the city and annexed it to the Greek state. Not all of Salonica's Jews were happy with this change of their city's status, from being an important provincial center of the Ottoman Empire to becoming a marginal provincial center of the new and rather small Greek nation-state, cut off from the Balkan hinterland. Substantial numbers left the city shortly after 1912, many of them, especially young men followed by their families, to avoid the military draft. Some moved to western Europe, to Paris, Vienna, Milan, Marseilles, Manchester, some as far away as New York, Mexico City, and Buenos Aires. Others more simply moved to Constantinople (Istanbul), where they continued to live under the impression that their mostly tranquil lives in Salonica could be reconstructed in the capital of the Ottoman Empire. Over time, this proved to be an illusion, but for Sephardic Jews in the 1910s, opting for the Ottoman Empire did not seem like a bad bet. After all, had not Kemal Ataturk himself been born and grown up in Salonica? Would not his leadership of the new Turkish state offer some continuity between the old world of Salonica and the Turkish Republic born out of the Empire's ashes?

Among those Salonican Jews who moved to Constantinople, there were two members of my more extended family: my grandmother Flora's sister, Bella, who, following her marriage, came to be known to us as *Madamme* Bella Botton, and my mother's uncle, Albert Alkalay. I remember them well from our visits to their homes in Turkey after the war. Over time, I grew close to *Oncle* Albert and *Tante* Lydia, his wonderful and very beautiful Russian Orthodox wife, a refugee from Kiev who escaped the aftermath of the Russian Revolution by mostly walking (!) to Istanbul where she met and married my great-uncle. My father's Turkish cousin, also named Albert, always pleasant and gregarious, and his vivacious red-haired Jewish wife Nellie, who hailed from Bursa in Asia Minor, also became close friends and in various moments of my later life gave me the benefit of their advice and support.

Memories of Salonica's Ottoman/Turkish past lingered for generations. Perhaps they still do. For my grandmother, born in 1876, and my father in 1899, this memory colored many aspects of their daily lives, most especially language, food, and music. My grandmother's daily consumption of coffee each morning (was it Greek or Turkish, her sons teased her) and of *kaïmaki* ice cream that the young waiter from the neighboring milk store would bring most every afternoon to *Mme.* Flore as he charmingly called her, kept these linguistic and alimentary residues very much a part of the social world of all Salonicans, Jews or not. I am always touched to discover, every time I visit my adult American-born daughter, whose itinerant life has taken her from New England in North America, to Tuscany, England, and most recently Wales, with short but frequent stays in Greece to spend time with her grandmother (my mother), that the most vivid evidence of her distant Selanikli Sephardic and Greek roots are the dishes she was taught by her grandmother, to whom she was very attached: *avgolemono* soup, *bourekakia*, *pasteliko*, and, still struggling to master it, *bouñouelos* (egg and lemon soup, cheese triangles, spinach pie, honey-dipped dough fritters). As for the remnants of Turkish music, its languid, characteristic sound penetrated and often transformed traditional Greek music, its tunes ever present in the city's streets and squares, in working-class joints and in restaurants frequented by wealthier patrons. As much as the tango was a sign of the city's "Europeanization," it remained a cultural import, competing with more indigenous and resilient forms of music and singing, and, of course, dancing.

Initially, after the city's incorporation into the Greek state, its multiethnic complexity persisted, Jews, Christians, and Muslims coexisting in tension among themselves but more or less peacefully. But in 1922, following yet another Greco-Turkish war that resulted in a catastrophic Greek defeat, the population's ethnic complexity was drastically changed. The city's Muslim inhabitants, including Jews who in the eighteenth century had been converted to Islam and were known as the *Dönme*, were mostly expelled from Greece and forcibly moved to Turkey, while Greek Orthodox inhabitants of Asia Minor and Eastern Thrace were themselves coerced to leave their homes, where they had often prospered for centuries. Mostly penniless, perhaps as many as one and a half million uprooted Greek Orthodox Christians, some of whom did not even speak Greek, were transferred to Greece and forced to find new homes in a country they had not known until then.

Of these, about a quarter of a million were settled in Salonica where it was hoped they would take over properties abandoned by the Muslims. Homeless, resentful about their horribly unjust fate, these refugees represented a new element in the city's population. Their presence reinforced the central government's determination to Hellenize Salonica. A central policy of all Greek governments from the 1920s until the present has been to give a purely Greek hue to the city's culture and to reinforce the notion that Salonica never, even during the centuries of Ottoman Turkish domination and of Jewish demographic predominance, had lost its Greek character. Tensions between the Greek Orthodox population and the city's Jews, who had lived there uninterruptedly for about five centuries, often marked the city's history in the twenty or so years before its occupation by the Germans in 1941. For generations, Jews had often felt themselves to be an integral, organic part of the city's history and culture; following 1912, but especially after 1922, they were made to feel that they were a minority, marginalized and at best tolerated by the city's Greek Orthodox population. The Zionist movement, which had attracted the sympathies of substantial numbers of Salonica's Jews, reinforced the sentiment of many Jews' alienation from their traditional *patria*.

Local Greeks greeted the refugees from Asia Minor with more than a smidgen of suspicion and condescension; they were different—indeed, many thought of them as inferior—from old Greece's Greeks, the common saying being that they were Turkish-seeded (τουρκόσποροι), there was something alien—Turkish—in their customs, their language, their ways of being. Yet, for all their real or perceived differences, the fact was that the attendance of both groups en masse at Greek Orthodox religious rituals created an inchoate sense of community that was reinforced every Sunday and greatly solidified at the time of solemn holidays, such as Christmas and Easter or the Assumption of the Virgin on 15 August. So, by and large, the resilient anti-Jewish sentiment that had persisted in Greek Orthodox lands for generations, was not diluted following the refugees' arrival in 1922. Only now in Salonica and in the surrounding areas, it was expressed by a much larger number of people, many of whom tended to ogle the properties of the Jews as possible compensation for the wealth they had lost at the time of their expulsion from Turkey.

The Shoah in its Salonican-Greek variant was consummated in a local context where intense rivalries between Christians and Jews were a constant presence in the city's life. With the silencing of a strong Jewish voice as a consequence of the Shoah, after the war, much of the Jewish legacy to Salonica's history was willfully forgotten. It was as if a huge sigh of relief was exhaled by the city's population—perhaps one should better say that a collective fit of amnesia overtook the city's leaders—intellectuals, secondary-school and university professors, public servants, newspaper editors and journalists, lawyers and notaries, doctors and pharmacists, not to speak of priests and bishops and other religious functionaries. Jews had now become a very, very small minority, from fifty, perhaps sixty, thousand to about two to three thousand people. Their properties, in circumstances that to this day have never been fully investigated, passed to the hands of Christians. Even the grounds of their cemetery—perhaps the largest Jewish one in Europe, larger it seems even than the one in Prague—had been assigned to the local university, where, for decades, rectors, deans, and faculty assemblies had stubbornly refused even to place a plaque commemorating the Jewish cemetery's presence in that spot. One of my troubling memories of those immediate postwar years was the sight of slabs of marble, marked by strange signs—Hebrew letters!—found in the most unlikely spots in the city. These mutilated tomb stones, scattered about when the Jewish cemetery was vandalized—it should be added not by the Germans but by local municipal authorities—were put to all sorts of uses: as paving stones to decorate church yards, as building materials to construct street pavements and sidewalks, and, in at least one case, to firm up the walls of a swimming pool.

So, in the years immediately after 1945, when following the wartime adventures that take up the better part of this book, together with my parents I returned to Salonica, Jews who had survived were often accepted as if they were unwelcome intruders. The true story, recounted innumerable times by my father, is indicative of conditions and of the mood that prevailed at the time. A young survivor filed a petition that the family business, which had been registered in his father's name, be transferred to his, as his father had never returned from Auschwitz. The response of the competent authorities was that the son's request could not be honored until he provided his father's death certificate. Antisemitism has all sorts of ways of expressing itself!

Jews were now surrounded by silence, with little curiosity expressed by neighbors, classmates, or others about the circumstances of their survival. In the two schools I attended from 1946 to1956, where the city's *bien-pensant* middle-class families sent their children, not once did a classmate, a teacher, or anyone else ever ask me the obvious question: Tony, how did you survive the war; how is it that you were able to make it back to Salonica, when so many other Jews never came back? As a good friend from my school days recently ruminated: Never were topics of this sort discussed at home. We did not ask, and parents never offered any information.

I confess that among my various aims in writing this book was to give a small answer to these questions. How were my family and I able to return to our home, when two of my grandparents, an uncle, an aunt, not to mention numerous other relatives were not given a chance to survive even for a couple of days when they were transported to Auschwitz, and when more than 45,000 Salonican Jews perished in concentration camps? And what happened to us in the war's aftermath?

An Old Man and His Younger Self

Many years—indeed, many decades—have passed since the events I describe in this book. At the beginning of this story, I was not quite four years old. Now, I am well past my eighty-third birthday. A whole lifetime lies between my two selves, and I can't help but wonder if the old man I am now is the same person I was in my early boyhood, when I lived in Salonica. Repeatedly, as I was writing these memories, I puzzled over this conundrum. One of the recurring themes in the pages that follow is the challenges an old man faces when he tries to remember his youth. In my case, everything around me has changed—the people whom I could interrogate about my memories are all dead. The buildings, and public squares where I spent my daily life are now unrecognizable, so profoundly have they been transformed. My *patria*, to the extent to which I may have one, is different from what it was when I was a boy. Everything has changed, not necessarily for the worse, as our newly acquired attachment to Europe shows. Yet, I still go by the same name I bore almost eighty years ago and in some ungraspable way my present self is a continuation of my old one. My own recollections are fragmented, and often what in retrospect seemed to be important—indeed crucial—details remain unrecognizable, enveloped in the mist of a distant past. What did my grandparents look like? I do not recall. The uncle who was responsible for my survival should occupy a privileged place in my memory. I can hardly remember him, and when I do it is mostly from pictures I saw when I was older. Indeed, as the reader will discover, photographs have helped me reconstruct key moments of my family life.

When I think of my past, these are the stories that first come to mind, they are the events that have shaped me more than perhaps I was willing to acknowledge for many years following my adolescence. Still, there is a question that persists in the background. The reader might quite correctly want to ask here: Whose stories are these, anyway? Better yet, whose memories am I recording? If the bulk of the stories I recounted date mostly from a short period of slightly more than two years—from March 1943 to April/May 1945—how I can I claim that they are my memories when at the beginning of this period I was not quite four years old and at its end not quite six? So, for my own and the reader's clarification, now that I have recorded these stories, I should make some things clear.

A good deal of what is contained in this book is not my own direct memory. I mean, I did not experience, but heard from others, some of the events I described. Others, indeed, I experienced but am uncertain about how my current memory of these events corresponds to the imprint they left on my mind at the time they happened. Remembering one's past many decades after the events recalled is a complicated business. Time has a way of playing all sorts of tricks: its apparent speed when one is old in contrast to its seemingly glacial cadences in the early years of one's life, the foreshortening of events, the shadows in which it envelops some happenings, or the sharpness with which it etches some others on one's mind. In the case of the memories I present here, I tried to weave together a story that draws into one tapestry—or, to be more prosaic, into one narrative—my memories, regardless of their origins. I would like to think that one of my daughters, who is a much-accomplished weaver, will not dislike my use of this metaphor: weaving strands of wool into a tapestry that has the appearance of one, aesthetically pleasing object. In some way, this has been my ambition, to learn from her skill and weave a story that is at once true and suggestive.

In the case of the stories I recounted, not only did I have no sense of their importance, I had no awareness of their contemporary historical context. But many details have stuck in my mind. So, in the body of this small book I record little stories of brief moments, separate in time and place from each other, that are lifted out of a broader flow of events. They are linked to each other only by the fact that, directly or indirectly, they refer to my family and to me, and to our experiences at a time when the normal course of family life had been violently disrupted. They form a sort of palimpsest, below which the outlines of a continuous and more significant story is discernible, one that impinged, often dramatically, on the lives of many people during the Axis occupation of Greece. As the reader will discover, these are stories of my parents' flight from Salonica, their spectacular getaway through occupied Greece, worthy of a script for a suspenseful movie, my mother's capture in a train traveling from Lamia to Athens and her nearly miraculous escape, their arrival in Athens, where my mother lived for the following two years, while my father, shortly after their arrival in Athens, joined the resistance forces, but only after waiting to ensure that I would myself reach Athens safely and a secure hiding place would be found for me. And, of course, running through this narrative—a sort of *basso continuo* I try to ensure the reader does not overlook—is my own small history, the ups and downs of a young boy's adventures, who, unbeknownst to himself, was being bounced hither and yon for reasons that were beyond his comprehension but whose cumulative result was to ensure his survival.

As I mulled over these issues, I often reflected on an idea Paul de Man once expressed, that it is not life itself that produces a text but rather the opposite: it is the text that produces life and defines that life's contours. However much I might detest de Man as a person and as an intellectual who collaborated with the Nazis in World War II and then concealed his collaboration from his academic colleagues and students in the United States, I can't but wonder if his insight about the relationship between life and a biography (or autobiography) might resonate with what I am trying to do here. Having finished the composition of this book, I can only admit that the picture of my early life that I now have in my mind is the fruit of this writing. Reluctantly, I concede to de Man an important point of method.

As I was writing this book, I also had to reflect on an issue that historians (and I happen to be one) have puzzled over in the recent past. In a much-discussed essay, the prominent French sociologist Pierre Bourdieu rather radically questioned the possibility that anyone—historian or not—could write a biographical or autobiographical account and "describe a life" as if it were a straight line, with a beginning, middle, and end (with the double meaning that the term "end" implies). Any (auto)biography, he argued, is a specious construct, the fruit of a narcissistic impulse. That is all well and good, and, at a later point in this book I shall reflect briefly on the challenge of cobbling together an account of one's (in this case, my) life over the span of a few years. There is no denying the fact that, as the reader will understand even by glancing at the book's table of contents, I did adopt a roughly chronological order in the presentation of my memories. If this order responds to a narcissistic impulse or not, it is up to the reader to judge. What I would simply (and no doubt naively) contend is that I had something to say about my past, and I have tried to say it in as simple and unadorned way I could. In short, I confess to my own limit of being unable to think about my early years (and not only these) as if they were detached from events that had happened earlier in my life. Chronology, therefore, returns with somewhat of a vengeance in the account that follows, *pace* Bourdieu.

Then there is the matter of words. What words to choose, and how to choose them, when trying to describe events that, in retrospect, have something unusual, perhaps even a touch of drama about them? Yet, as far as I remember, when these events happened, they did not strike me as anything more than part of a daily routine that seemed to be unremarkable. Is there a language that captures at once a very young boy's naivety and

COURAGE AND COMPASSION

ignorance and an old man's marvel that such events could have taken place and that the protagonist of these stories was a very different persona of who he is today, as he is struggling to write these lines? The choice of words, especially in a language that is not my *langue maternelle*, is a tricky business. But English is the one language that, over the past sixty or so years, I have tried to learn how to write and that my most immediate family members—spread out as we are from Greece, Italy, England, Wales, France, Holland, Turkey to the United States—can read with some ease. Hence, the decision to write in English, and the struggle to pick out of my persistently imperfect mastery of this language words and expressions that suit my purpose. As it is, readers will judge these memories for what they are: strands of a distant past that may cast some light not necessarily only on my life and the world in which I lived in my early years but also bring into somewhat sharper focus some of the broader circumstances in which I grew up.

So, the old man struggles to remember and struggles even harder to distinguish the sources of his memories. Yet, in the process of writing, some patterns seemed to have emerged in my mind. These patterns are surely related to the German occupation and the upheavals it brought to our lives. Not that I remember much about the occupation. But I do have very clear images of the violent changes the Germans caused to my family and to me, personally. Thinking about it all, time and again I am struck by the zigzags of my childhood years, by the shifts in family surroundings, as (depending on how one counts) five or six times during a span of less than two years I was moved from one family to another, in an effort to keep me at arm's length from the fate the Nazis had promised to all Jews, young and old. The unusual times I lived through when I was a little boy have remained in my mind, mostly in small details that left a deep impression on me back then and often continue to do so now. The stories in this book regard the life of a young Jewish boy and of his family at the time when being Jewish was a challenge, the risks were ever present, the chances of getting through physically unscarred were long shots, at best. Without claiming any credit for my survival, the fact is that I did survive, against the odds; my survival was mostly the outcome of the selflessness and goodness of others as much as of good luck.

But beyond the survival of some and the death of many more (in the case of my immediate family, my mother was the only survivor on her side, the rest of her immediate family had all been murdered in Auschwitz), a point struck me very forcefully as I was writing this book: the long afterlife of the Shoah and of its weight on those who survived. Arguably, as I suggest in the book's last chapters, nearly everything important that my parents, sister, and I did after the war was an attempt to reconcile ourselves to the memory of the Shoah and to try, mostly unsuccessfully it turns out, to normalize its influence on our lives. There was no return to prewar normalcy after 1945, just the slow unfolding of the war's consequences, which lasted for decades, until my parents' death and my own slow decline into the decrepitude of old age.

In this sense, I think all members of my family would have agreed with a statement by Saul Friedlander, himself the author of a splendid book of his wartime memories: "I am a Jew, albeit without any religion or tradition-related attachments, indelibly marked by the Shoah. Ultimately, I am nothing else" (*When Memory Comes*, 1979). In this sentence, the adverb "ultimately," seems to me to be the key qualifier. There is no room in this adverb for the weight of national categories, none for all those varied experiences that, cumulatively, shaped us into being who we are. However important, these were temporary, even evanescent events. But the Shoah stands apart in its immensity as an event and as a memory, its shadow not faded over time on the consciousness and on the unfolding lives of those who remember it.

The misadventures of one Jewish child during the years of Europe's Nazi domination is a far from uncommon story. Over the past half century or more, a number of books and memoirs have been written on such stories. In its basic outlines, my story is not so different. Of course, the details differed, and some of these details might be worth writing about. But each such memoir often seems to me to be a variation of the same theme, an often lachrymose, awe-struck retelling of a tragic, even heroic adventure. I can think only of a few exceptions to this generalization. Was it possible to think of another way of presenting such a story? Slowly, as I grappled with this challenge, I was tempted by the idea of using the example of my childhood years as an occasion to reflect upon a larger problem that has preoccupied me over the years: The position of Jews in Greek society in the decades on either side of World War II. My intention was not to write a history of Christian-Jewish relations in Salonica, the town where I was born and to which, even today, I feel emotionally attached in ways that are not easy to describe. This is a task that others have addressed, and will no doubt continue to explore. Mine merely turned out to be a personal testimony, a reflection of someone who, over several years, chose to spend some of his time pondering the problems a Jew of his generation faced—or thought he faced—while growing up in Greece.

The stories, as well as the sundry reflections I present here, often converge on two issues: memory and boundaries. Time and again as I was writing this small book, I had to interrogate myself about the nature of my memories, their sources, their survival, or their re-emergence in my consciousness after many decades. I confess to not fully understanding the process by which writing and remembering interact with each other. It seemed to me that often in their interaction they teased out of my mind (or, perhaps, out of my subconscious) small truths from the past. The other issue that recurs in the pages that follow has to do with the boundaries between Jewish and Greek (or, better, Greek Orthodox) life in Salonica, and more generally in Greece, in the years around 1940, and the ease or difficulty of crossing these boundaries. In that place and time, what it meant to be a Jew raised complex issues, and these stories illustrate, if only indirectly, that complexity—as I perceive it now, many decades following the events I describe. But the issue of boundaries—their resilience or their porousness—has loomed large in my mind throughout my adult life, and it is from this perspective that I am looking back on my early years.

Note

1. All figures are provided by the author and used with permission.

2.
Being Greek

Before being carried off to be murdered in Auschwitz, Uncle Richard (pronounced with a soft "ch" and stress on the second syllable), my mother's brother, had a Christian lover. Their relationship lasted several years with two children, a son and a daughter, born to it. In the very early 1940s, he and his companion probably traveled to Albania to legitimate their union in a civil ceremony. After the war, my mother fiercely denied that such a marriage ever took place. It could not, she said, because the mother of her brother's children was Greek. She meant Greek Orthodox but said only Greek. After the war, I don't remember her name being mentioned in the family, at least not in my presence. She was simply referred to in Ladino as *la griega*, someone from another universe. Even though over time I came to recognize her whenever she would come to plead with my father for a part of her husband/lover's inheritance, I do not think I spoke to her even once. Her children, Erricos, older by a year or two than me, and Niki (Victory), a year younger than me, born, as her name suggests in 1940, the year of the Greco-Italian war, never were part of our street gang, even though they were Christian, and I the only Jewish child in the group. Whenever reference was made to Richard, my parents, especially my mother, would draw a firm line between our family and the *griegos*. Yet, that fact does not account for my father's occasional, far from infrequent, under the table payments to my uncle's widow, to help her make ends meet. I do not know how often these payments were made. I suspect they were more frequent and more substantial than my father would have wanted to acknowledge to my mother, although in those circumstances, a certain amount of dissimulation might have been at work, as my father concealed these payments from my mother, while she feigned she was not aware of them.

Even if not much was said about my uncle, his photograph, in Greek Army uniform at the Albanian front in winter 1940–41, was a reminder to all visitors in our sitting-room, that not only had he existed but through him our family had contributed to Greece's war effort. The family disdained his personal life because he had breached imagined boundaries of bourgeois Jewish respectability. But the family seemed to have no second thoughts about showing his photograph in army uniform, with symbols of the Greek state including a decoration perhaps won on the field, where guests could admire it in the family parlor. In the years after the war, the case of Mordechaios Frizis, a Jew from Chalkida, and the first Greek Army officer to have fallen on the Albanian front soon after the Italian invasion in late October 1940, was hardly known to Salonican Jews. Not until much later, in official Greek government pronouncements and in celebratory statements of the Jewish community, was Frizis presented as a symbol of the presumed symbiosis between Christians and Jews in Greece, a Greek citizen who sacrificed his life for the protection of the fatherland. For us, Uncle Richard's photograph did not carry any such symbolic value. He was a member of the family who, resident as he was in Greece, and

Figure 2.1. *Uncle Richard, my mother's brother, in the mid-1920s. He was murdered in Auschwitz.*

born a year before Salonica became Greek, had no choice but to obey the government's orders to respond to the call for arms. His service in uniform had not spared his life, and like thousands of other Salonican Jews, he was transported to Auschwitz where he was murdered a few days following his arrival there. For us, in the years after the war, rather than a symbol, Uncle Richard's picture posed a question. Were we Greeks who happened to be Jews, in which case we could properly take pride in my uncle's feats in wartime? Or were we simply Jews who happened to live in Greece, which might conceivably justify my mother's harsh stance toward her nephew and niece? These questions did not much occupy me then. They have been very much on my mind in the last several years.

In our daily lives, and in the culture that was transmitted from my elders to the young, it was made clear that we were different. At home, our languages were different. We seldom spoke Greek; Ladino, French, and, later, English were our languages of communication. The piles of books in various corners of the house were all in French, English, Italian, even in German, which my father knew well but was reluctant to use after the war. To my teachers' irritation and amusement, the *Grande Encyclopédie Larousse* served me more than adequately whenever I had to chase down some information for a school assignment. We did not have a Greek encyclopedia in the house. Nor do I remember many books in Greek, although when I was about ten years old (or, perhaps, a little older) I did read *The Odyssey*, Aesop, and some other ancient Greek classics in French translation. Both my parents had an excellent command of Greek—oral and written; but they used it mostly outside the house, in my father's business, and their volunteer work for the Jewish community, which required frequent contact with state and municipal authorities. As for me, it was Greek with my friends outside the house and with the household help, French with my parents, and Ladino with my grandmother, who could read only in Ladino, but then again only if it was written in Hebrew characters.

I don't remember any of us having any trouble shifting from one of these languages to another nor did we confuse one with the others. A sort of linguistic *macédoine* prevailed at home and in family gatherings, and it set us apart from neighbors and acquaintances whose monolingual regimens we, I mean my sister, cousins, and I, sometimes childishly envied. What, then, was our *langue maternelle*? By all accounts, it was that amalgam of languages that prevailed in our conversations at home. Perhaps this is the reason—although I suspect this is a lame excuse—that although I think I know these languages well, I cannot claim to have mastered any of them.

Our infrequent visits to the synagogue were reminders of our apartness. On occasional Friday evenings, when my mother with an aunt or friend would visit the synagogue to offer olive oil to the lamp in memory of the dead, I accompanied her and listened respectfully to the rabbi's or cantor's chants as my mother would fumble through her bag for a handkerchief with which I could cover my head. *Kippas* were very hard to find in Salonica in the years immediately after the war, and I remember how envious I was when I saw someone of my generation wearing one, probably sent by a relative in the United States or some other country. I think I went along to these ritual visits rather happily in the first years following the war—no problem leaving behind my neighborhood friends who would continue their play while I, scrubbed and well dressed, followed my mother to the synagogue. Later, especially when I had started seeing friends after school, I resisted my mother's invitation to be, as she would on occasion try to flatter me, her *chevalier*. Until the mid-1950s when together with my family I moved to the United States, the constant reminders of what had happened to us during the war reinforced my sense of difference; after all, my mother's father, mother, brother, sister, and numerous other relatives were murdered in Auschwitz, or they died on the way to their final destination because of the bestial conditions in the trains that carried them to the concentration camps.

For years, on Yom Kippur at the synagogue, the women's wailing and the men's quiet crying drove deep into my consciousness the notion that there was something special in our recent history; it was different from that of my classmates and neighborhood chums. I well remember my first Yom Kippur services in the Monastyriotòn synagogue in the autumn of 1945, shortly after our return to Salonica and just after my sixth birthday. Of the few dozen synagogues that had existed in the city before the war, it was the only one left standing by the Germans and their local minions. The two thousand or so Jews who had returned to the city that spring and summer were jammed in a space that could perhaps have accommodated a few hundred people. I walked toward the synagogue holding my father's hand. I do not think my mother was with us; those were the days when she had suffered a nervous breakdown and remained confined to bed. No sooner had we reached the neighborhood of the synagogue than I was struck by everyone's seriousness, even more so by the severity of my uncles' looks and their uncharacteristically unsmiling faces. To say that the atmosphere was heavy is an understatement. You could hardly breathe and barely move among the crowd that had been forced to stand, after all the seats were taken. Initially, I was allowed to sit downstairs with my father and his two brothers. A little later, having spotted my grandmother peering out from the balcony upstairs, I was sent to sit with the women. I pushed my way up a narrow and winding stairwell through the wall of women and reached my grandmother in the front row. But soon thereafter a loud, collective cry rose from the assembled worshippers. Sitting on my grandmother's lap, I was dazed by the spectacle of all those people shouting, crying, praying out loud, protesting the murder of so many relatives, neighbors, and friends. My grandmother, sensing my fear, gently slid me off her lap and urged me to return downstairs to the men's company. The experience of that Yom Kippur service and of the pandemonium in the synagogue deeply marked me for a long time. It was my introduction to the commemoration of the Shoah.

Just weeks before, I had started school, enrolled in the first grade of a Greek private school. Not one of my classmates had shared that Yom Kippur experience. I was the only Jewish boy in my class, one of a handful in the school. My difference from my classmates and from all the neighborhood children whom I had gotten to know in the previous few months was evident to me. A significant part of my life was spent in a separate universe, and no one—I mean, absolutely no one—had expressed any interest at all in hearing from me about that universe. Of course, I socialized easily with friends and classmates. I could play with them in the schoolyard and in the street, I was even invited into the homes of a few. But all this was done as long as I did not open my mouth and say something about my different experiences or about the special occasions when I would follow my parents to the synagogue or, rarer still, to the Jewish cemetery. How could I, a Jewish boy, feel that I was Greek when my friends were indifferent to a part of my experience that so sharply distinguished us, when State and Church and often friends and neighbors, even my favorite teachers, reinforced my sense of apartness?

It was not always easy to find an answer to this question. Another incident, probably in 1947, although I am unsure of the year, underscored some of the contradictions and tensions that I felt. On a sunny Sunday afternoon, I was told to put on my good clothes because we would visit the synagogue. To my amazement, as we got close, I saw the streets lined with soldiers in dress uniform while dozens of other people, evidently not Jews because they did not enter the synagogue, were standing quietly on the sidewalks. Greek flags were flying at half-mast along the street, and a military band was waiting for the captain's command to start playing. As we entered, we passed by a few Greek Orthodox priests, bedecked in their ceremonial garb chanting their prayers, while the cantor stood further back, in front of the bimah. It was then that my father explained to me what was going on. A young man, a Jew from Salonica, on active service in the Greek armed forces, had been killed when the truck on which he was riding somewhere in the countryside was blown up by a mine planted by members of the communist insurgence. I did not understand anything at all of the adults' conversation about the civil war, the communist-inspired forces that were occupying much of the Greek countryside, or the Greek Army fighting their insurgency. But I did hear a friend of my father's say to him that it was a terrible pity for a young man, who had been saved from the Nazis, to have met such a terrible death. I did not at all comprehend my father's response: there were so few of us left, and we should protect the young. I understood that the "we" referred to us, Jews. How could we be so few, I wondered, when such a crowd had gathered at the synagogue that day? The solemnity and sadness of that funeral ceremony, the rabbi's and the priests' Hebrew and Greek chanting, the evident displeasure in my mother's face at the presence of Greek priests, the patriotic tone of the funeral orations delivered by a Greek Army officer and by a member of the Jewish Community Council were all mingled in my mind as strains of a confused amalgam of different stories I did not know what to make of. How could a small child, a passive witness to that ceremony, tell the difference between Greek and Jewish cultures, mingled as they were in the rituals of that Sunday afternoon? The sounds of the military band playing (as I found out later) Chopin's Funeral March as the coffin of the unfortunate young soldier was carried onto a military truck waiting outside the synagogue added to the mixture of sounds and sights that puzzled, perhaps even intrigued me on that sunny Sunday afternoon. Where was my place in that world, where so many often contradictory traditions pushed and pulled me this way and that? Was there a solid ground on which I could stand and understand who I was?

My mixed feelings were reinforced on an Easter Sunday, I think in 1946 (although perhaps it was a year later). During our forced absence from our home in Evzonon Street from March 1943 to April 1945, various apartments in our building, left empty by their Jewish tenants, had been occupied by Christians, refugees either from the Greco-Turkish war of 1922 or from the countryside surrounding Salonica, which had been devastated in the years immediately following 1945 during the civil war. In strictly legal terms, these new neighbors were intruders, abusively occupying their small apartments. But when we returned, my parents managed to strike reasonably good relations with them, and some of the refugee women were on occasion called upon by my mother to help out with cooking when important guests came over for lunch. Takis, *Kyra* Mariò's son, was a boy about my age, a new neighbor, who quickly became a good friend. He, and a bunch of other boys (I don't think there was a single girl in the gang) opened up their circle to me, and I remember endless hours of playing and horsing around with them. A day or two before Easter Sunday, Takis, almost certainly encouraged by his mother, asked me to join him and his family for Easter Sunday Liturgy, at the Church of the Holy Trinity a couple of blocks from home. Flattered by the invitation, I ran to my parents to inform them and ask for their permission. I distinctly remember their puzzled looks, but my mother broke the ice and, speaking in Ladino, told my father to let the *niño* go with his friends.

Figure 2.2. *The street gang on Evzonon Street. I took this photograph myself sometime in the early 1950s with a camera given me as a present by Uncle Mousa. My sister, Marcella, who had been born in 1946, is sitting in the middle of the front row.*

COURAGE AND COMPASSION

So, on a bright Sunday morning, dressed up in my very finest, I found myself sitting through a long and, to me, boring Mass. The ritual was vaguely familiar to me because of my wartime experience, which I shall describe in a later chapter. What was not familiar and took me by surprise was the priest's sermon. Now I assume, without having a firm recollection, that he expatiated on the mysteries of the Crucifixion and Resurrection, topics beyond my understanding that left me indifferent. I had been following distractedly, puzzling over some of his points, my mind mostly floating away to look at the imposing chandelier that hung from the ceiling. All of a sudden, his words caught my attention. He was talking about Jews. By then I knew I was one. The preacher's vehemence and his message stunned me. He said something about the murderous Jews who were responsible for Christ's death. And as he was shouting his message, with his finger he seemed to be pointing in my direction as he urged his flock to expel Jews from their company, to rid society of their presence. They were vile and disgusting people. I was lost. Why would he be so cross at me and my parents? What had we done to arouse his anger? My instinctive reaction was that he could not be talking about me. So, I turned around and, looking over my shoulder, tried to spot any other Jews in the crowd. I could not see any. So, despondently, I concluded that, in the end, he could not but be talking about me and my family. His message was a mystery to me. After Mass, as we were walking home, Takis's parents did not mention anything about the priest's sermon. And I, sensing that it was best not to ask questions, sullenly returned home with them. I said nothing to my parents about my puzzlement. As time went on, I often thought about this incident and realized that, for all of Takis's friendship and his parents' cordial attitude to me, the priest's odious message (remember, we were one or two years following the extermination of between forty-five and fifty thousand of Salonica's Jews) conveyed exactly the ideology that did not, could not, allow me to feel Greek—fully Greek, no questions asked, no qualifications drawn. Time and again, in the years of my adolescence, the same message was driven home to me. I still remember my shock when, at about the age of sixteen, responding to my favorite teacher's questions as to what profession I would follow after my high school studies, I heard him say that as a Jew the doors of a certain profession I had mentioned to him were not open to me. But I shall return with more details to this incident below.

In the end, for one Jewish boy, born in Salonica just before the war, what it meant to be Greek involved mastering the country's language and its history, participating in national rituals and ceremonies (I remember once wearing an evzone uniform and another time parading with my classmates and saluting the flag and the state authorities on the day of national independence), cheering for the national soccer team, and absorbing as much of the dominant culture as I could. Until my fifties, the most indelible and deeply rooted evidence of my Greekness was my inability to count, in simple or complex ways, in any language other than Greek! However strong the forces and seemingly attractive the rewards of immersing myself in Greek culture, one element stood in the way of feeling fully Greek: the conviction, shared by family and overwhelmingly by non-Jewish acquaintances, that being Greek meant being Christian. During the war, hidden as I was, first, in a Catholic convent in Athens and then by a family that prayed in a Uniate Church, I participated in masses and occasionally as an altar boy, both in Catholic and Orthodox/Uniate religious rituals. In those years, very few Jewish boys in other parts of Europe are known to have converted to Christianity and then, in some cases, reverted to Judaism after the war. One thinks of the historian Saul Friedlander, the biblical scholar Geza Vermes, perhaps most strikingly, Jean-Marie Lustiger, although he did not revert to Judaism but went on to become a priest and eventually the bishop and cardinal of Paris. I suspect that not many Greeks, whether Jews or Christians, can boast such an eclectic religious experience! But eclectic experiences do not offer entry into a Greek community that is intensely proud of its national unity and often (to this day!) flaunts its racial purity. Sadly, I think that the preceding thought applies almost as much to most postwar Jews, as to Greeks who are Christian.

Another family story evokes different images and leads to other reflections. Another uncle and the woman he loved were protagonists of this story, as well. In the mid-1930s, one of my father's five brothers left Salonica to work in French Africa. The Greek Orthodox woman he had met in Salonica soon followed him to Conakry. There she prevailed on him to convert, and they were married in a Greek Orthodox church. I must have first met Uncle Maurice (Moussa in the family) and Aunt Keti in the late 1940s, during the first of several postwar visits to Salonica. To us, he and his family carried about them a different aura. Their stories about life in Conakry were bracingly entertaining, their travels through Africa and Europe on their way to Greece sounded exotic, the degree of comfort they took for granted in their daily lives set them apart from us. So did their self-assurance about the world and life in general.

Uncle Moussa's departure from Salonica conformed to our family's recent history. In the decades before the war, other close relatives, both on my father's and mother's sides, had left Salonica and settled in places as near as Istanbul, Alexandria,

Milan, and Paris, and as far away as Buenos Aires, Mexico City, and, it was once suggested to me, Montevideo. Uncle Moussa's departure from the family's religious (but was it only religious?) traditions was surely related to his physical distance from Salonica. This was also the case with other relatives who had similarly left their birthplace. His decision was similar to that of my mother's uncle in Istanbul, who married my much beloved Aunt Lydia, a Ukrainian, Russian Orthodox refugee from the Russian Revolution, or that of Colette, a second cousin of my mother's whom I never met and who, born in Salonica but settled in Paris when she was a small girl, married an immigrant from Dakar. My first wife, a Catholic woman whom I married in the United States, conformed to this pattern. Such behavior was tolerated from Jewish relatives who had settled in faraway places. But it was unusual for one of the Molhos who remained in Salonica to have married a non-Jew. The wave of intermarriages between my Molho cousins who grew up in Salonica and their Christian spouses did not begin until the 1970s, thirty years or more after the war's end.

More to the point, Uncle Moussa had crossed a huge barrier. Not only had he not married a Jew, for his wife's sake he gave the appearance of having forsaken Judaism. Yet, as far as I can recall, there was no tension or any unpleasantness about receiving them and my two cousins in our homes. To the contrary, all Molho households competed with each other to welcome them and host lavish lunches and dinners for them and for Aunt Keti's Christian relatives. Although, so as not to irritate his mother (my grandmother), Uncle Moussa did not flaunt his Christian convictions (if he had any), the fact is that he occasionally went to church with his wife. On one occasion, with my parents' consent, they took me to church on a Sunday. Uncle Moussa's branch of the Molho family had become Greek. Unlike Uncle Richard, Uncle Moussa did not seem in the family's eyes to have breached any boundary of respectability. Issues of belonging, of who was accepted in the family, who was not, and who was only partly and surreptitiously accepted, were resolved obliquely on the basis of ambiguous, perhaps even contradictory criteria. Even so, for all the ambiguity of Uncle Moussa's standing in the family, it seems to me that there was no question in anyone's mind that he and his family were living in a separate universe, far (not only geographically) from our own rather small and parochial, if discombobulated, Jewish world. As I think about it now, there is a sad irony to Uncle Moussa's experience. Toward the end of his life, he and Aunt Keti separated, and as the years passed, and he became older, he expressed a desire to formally be recognized as a Jew. Above all, he said on more than one occasion that he wished to be buried in a Jewish cemetery—in Athens (where he lived) or in Salonica. But he never pressed the issue vigorously, the Jewish Community of Salonica put a series of barriers to the realization of his request, and, in the end, he died before his wish was granted. So, in the end, to the deep disappointment and embarrassment of his only surviving brother (Uncle Roufa), but, as I suspect, to the relief of his two children, he received a Christian funeral and burial. Jews could be just as inflexible in judging who could or could not cross the barrier between the two religious communities.

The postwar fortress-like conviction about the separation of *griegos* and *jidios* was not my mother's alone, although in her case it was especially pronounced in the fifteen to twenty years following the war's end. It marked the views of many Salonican Jews following the traumatic years of the early 1940s. While it is true that in the preceding decades government policies had often reinforced this mentality, in the interwar decades, small breaches in this defensive stance had also been opened. On the one hand, there was an effort to keep Jews and non-Jews apart—for example, following the great fire of 1917, the creation of distinct neighborhoods where especially poor Jews lived, the establishment of separate electoral districts for the Jews so that their political preferences could be more carefully monitored; on the other hand, at least to judge from my family's experience, it became possible for Jews to strike reasonably warm social and business relations with Greek Orthodox neighbors and business associates.

There are two pieces of evidence that suggest I may be right on this score: a photograph (my parents' wedding picture) and a name (mine).

My parents' wedding picture hangs prominently on a wall in my house. Visitors to my home invariably ask me about it, struck as they are by the formality of the pose, and by the air of understated opulence and optimism that exudes from this picture. Taken in May 1937 in a professional photographer's studio, the picture celebrates, in terms that were recognizable by any successful middle-class family, the happy occasion of the wedding of Saul, son of Lazar (or Elazar) Molho and Flora Hasson, and Lily Alkalay, daughter of Nissim Alkalay and Henrietta Alkalay. (Nissim had been Henrietta's uncle, so, at the time of their wedding, both had the same family name.) The circumstances surrounding my parents' marriage are interesting in themselves, and they are worth briefly recounting.

The picture's happy smiles and studied harmony between the newlyweds conceal the stormy beginnings of their encounter. Sometime in the autumn of 1936, following a dinner in my maternal grandparents' home, when one of my grandfather's

Figure 2.3. *My parents' wedding picture, May 1937. Liolia Christidou, our neighbor, sits in front of the newlyweds.*

business associates and his family had been invited for dinner, as my mother and her mother were cleaning up, my mother was informed that this business associate's eldest son, Saul Molho, was chosen to become her husband. My mother's initial reaction was violent. She, marry someone whom she had just met, just because her father wanted her to marry him, even though he was so evidently older than she was? (It turned out that he was sixteen years older!) How could her father dare suggest that she interrupt her piano lessons when all her teachers at the Conservatory thought she had a brilliant musical future before her? Stop her piano and marry someone she had never met be-

Figure 2.4. *My mother's graduation picture from Anatolia College, 1934. She stands fourth from right.*

fore? None of this fitted her own upbringing and all the lessons she had learned in her French and American schooling! While her mother kept quiet during this intense confrontation and her brother kept needling her about her future, her father insisted. Saul Molho was a very good match, he was cultured, had his own successful business, and his family was well known and highly respected. The next day, following a new confrontation, the father suggested a compromise; if, after a few months, Lily did not like her pre-selected spouse, she would be free to call the whole thing off. It turns out that the two rather got along well, as my mother's vivacious and more spontaneous personality complemented my father's quieter and more pensive inclination. So, the wedding was never called off and was celebrated in May 1937.

A handwritten document, interestingly found among Uncle Isaac's papers some years after his death in the summer of 1983, sheds light on my parents' wedding. The details of this prenuptial contract no doubt follow the tradition of arrangements for middle-class Jewish marriages in prewar Salonica. Written in Ladino in *solitreo* (Hebrew cursive script) and dated December 1936 (the date is not entirely clear on this manuscript agreement), the document was signed by my two grandparents who agreed that the "young and prominent" Saul, son of the "wise and splendid Elazar Molho" and the "virgin Lily, daughter of the wise and splendid Nissim Alkalay" would marry each other; and that a dowry of 375,000 drachmas (by my calculation, worth at the time about 1,000 golden English sovereigns) would be

Figure 2.5. *My parents at the time of their engagement, February 1937.*

given to the groom by the bride's father, 50,000 of which would be paid fifteen days before the wedding. The characterizations of the four persons mentioned in this document—Saul Molho and his father Elazar, Lily Alkalay and her father Nissim—are formulaic and appear in many (if not all) such prenuptial agreements. The document bears three signatures, those of my two grandfathers, and a third indecipherable one, probably that of a rabbi or witness.

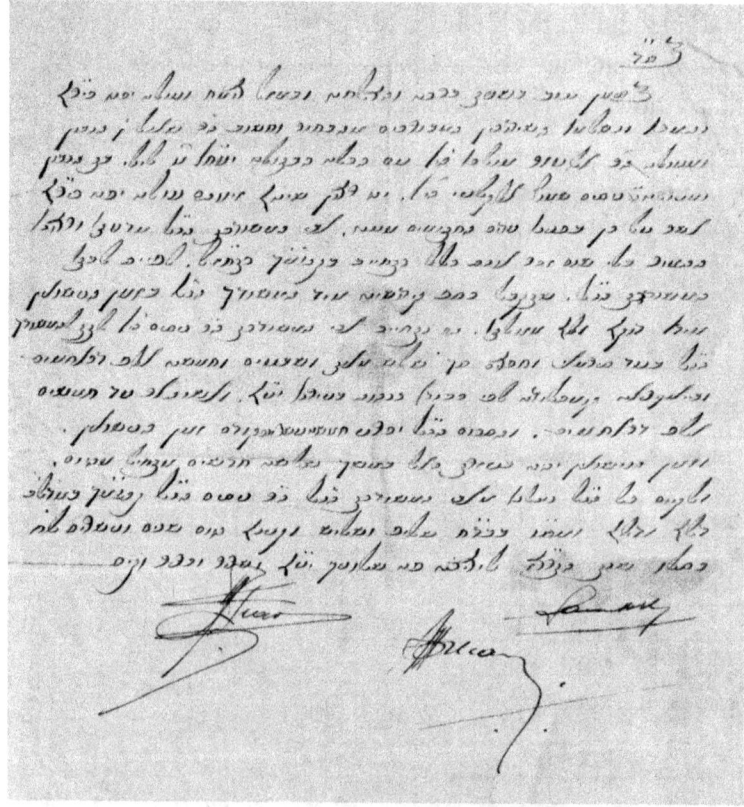

Figure 2.6. *Marriage contract for my parents' wedding, December 1936. It was written in Ladino, in solitreo script.*

COURAGE AND COMPASSION

None of this tension and the negotiations that no doubt preceded the wedding are revealed in my parents' wedding picture. As pictures most often do, they capture static moments when time is frozen; in this case, this picture conveys a moment of serenity, even happiness. The groom, wearing a formal black suit and holding a pair of white gloves, stands somewhat stiffly next to his bride, a trace of self-satisfied smile softening the reserve that was deeply ingrained in his character. My mother, radiant in her impressive wedding gown, with an elegant white floral crown on her head, holds a large bouquet of white flowers and smiles pleasantly to the camera. In addition to the bride and groom, the photograph includes also the picture of a flower girl. Dressed herself in a very fine, long, white dress, the young lady sits at my mother's feet, enveloped in the bride's white gown. By her looks she must have been about eight or nine years old. It turns out that her name was Liolia Christidou, daughter of a prominent lawyer, whose family lived directly across the street from us. Liolia and her parents must have attended my parents' wedding ceremony in my grandparents' synagogue. They must also have been present at the reception hosted by my mother's father in one of the city's fine restaurants.

I am unsure if Mr. Christides had been a close friend of my grandparents. His daughter's presence in such a prominent role at the time of my parents' wedding shows that, in the years before the immense upheaval that overtook Salonica a few years later, good, even cordial relations could be cultivated between two families—one Jewish, the other Christian.

Then, there is the case of my parents' choice of my name: Antonis, a non-Jewish name if ever there was one, Roman in origin but widely also used by Christians, both Orthodox and Catholic. They couldn't have known that my name would have significant consequences for my future. My parents' decision to give me a non-Jewish name suggests the range of possibilities about how Salonica's Jews—in this instance, members of a middle-class, well-educated family—could relate to Christian Orthodox Greeks in the years immediately before the war.

If I had been born thirty or forty years earlier, there was no chance whatsoever that my parents would have chosen this name for me. Suffice to look at two sets of pictures, also in my possession, to get a sense of a big cultural shift among Salonica's Jews in the first half of the twentieth century. The first set of pictures shows the parents of my father's mother. My great-grandfather's long, white beard, and the fez-like cap on his head, and his wife's heavy matronly garments, among which, since I was a child, I could not help but be struck by her furs and her bonnet-

Figure 2.7. *(a) My maternal great-grandmother, and also (b) My maternal great-grandfather. I do not know their names. Both pictures were probably taken in the early years of the twentieth century.*

like hat, were typical of the traditional garb worn by Salonica's Sephardic Jews for generations before these pictures were taken, I guess (without having any proof about this) in the early years of the twentieth century.

Then, there is the second set of pictures, those of the first couple's daughter (my father's mother) and her husband (my grandfather). Their photographic portraits could just as well have been of any middle-aged European bourgeois couple in the interwar years. If my grandfather's looks bespeak his conservative temperament and his often dour appearance, my grandmother's understated elegance, and the pleasant smile on her slim face contrast sharply with her mother's heavy-set features. Somewhere between the styles of these two sets of pictures is a third nice portrait of my mother, aged about three, with her par-

Figure 2.8. *(a) My paternal grandfather, Lazar Molho, son of Saul, and (b) My paternal grandmother Flora Hasson. Both pictures were taken in the 1920s or 1930s.*

ents, and her brother (Uncle Richard). Taken around the year 1918, it shows my grandmother wearing the traditional Sephardic long dress, sitting next to her husband, dressed in a nicely cut European suit. To the left of my grandparents stands their seven-year-old son, wearing a spiffy boys' sailor suit, while, to their right, my mother, in her cute European-style dress, looks puzzlingly to the camera. European styles had entered my grandparents' home, although my grandmother's appearance suggests that this movement of dressing styles from West to East had not taken place without some resistance.

Salonica had changed greatly in the interwar decades, and the city's Jews reacted variously to the often contradictory political and cultural pressures to which they were exposed. On the one hand, there was the ever-clear pressure of popular antisemitism, often seconded by government authorities, intended to diminish and marginalize Jewish influence in the city. Yet, social life also made it possible for Jews and Christians to cultivate contacts between them and become familiar with each other's customs and traditions. Some middle-class Jews and Christians could and did socialize in clubs and cafés, where they occasionally met; working class Jews and Christians shared aspirations, while both joined the activities of the city's socialist movement (Federassion Sosialista Ovradera), the first socialist movement anywhere in the Ottoman Empire, founded by Avrom Benaroya, a Bulgarian Sephardic Jew who had settled in Salonica. There were also obvious pressures to Hellenize the city's Jews. Jewish children now were instructed in Greek, even in the foreign, European schools where middle-class Jews had sent their children for the previous two or three generations. School excursions were organized to "old Greece," where students and their teachers were introduced to the marvels of ancient Athe-

Figure 2.9. *The Alkalay family. The photograph was taken in 1917 or 1918, in the Antonio Porcessi Studio. My grandfather Nissim stands, my grandmother Henrietta, wearing the half traditional dress, sits, my Uncle Richard and my mother stand.*

nian civilization, which, they were instructed, was one of the two pillars of modern Greek culture, the other being the Greek Orthodox Church. A picture of my mother, aged about sixteen, shows her standing on the Acropolis with other schoolgirls her age. In the generation before the war, the lines that separated my mother's family from her Greek neighbors were almost certainly softer and more porous than she herself was willing to admit after 1945.

My mother's postwar harsh judgment about relations between Christians and Jews does not help explain her and my father's choice of my name. The choice grew out of my maternal grandfather's friendship with his doctor. My grandfather, Nissim Alkalay (the father of my Uncle Richard, my mother, and my mother's younger sister, Marcella), was a prosperous wholesale dry goods merchant in Salonica but suffered with heart trouble. His doctor, Antonios Vaïnanidis, nursed him back to good health after each one of his periodic crises. I do not know when and under what circumstances my maternal grandfather met and befriended him. But the fact is that Dr. Antonios Vaïnanidis and Nissim Alkalay were good enough friends to convince my parents to give me the doctor's name. My mother bore me, so at least I was told, following one of these crises. And so, by an almost unbelievable stretch of the imagination in the sort of Jewish family I was born into, as a gesture of a patient's profound friendship for his doctor, I was given the name of my grandfather's good friend. I was named Antonios, unmistakably a non-Jewish—more significantly, a Roman and Greek Christian—name.

By any contemporary standard, this was not a simple decision. Arguably it had broken a deeply entrenched precedent and caused some tension in the family. A younger friend of mine, who is able to read the *solitreo* script in which Judeo-Spanish was very often written, dug up my birth registration in the microfilmed copies of the records of the Salonican Jewish community's archive (whose originals are located in Moscow, but that is another story). There, my name is registered as "Elazar (Antonios)." Yet, about a year later, in my father's family declaration (probably for tax purposes) in the community, my name is simply listed as "Antonios." My paternal grandparents almost certainly had expected me to be named Elazar or Lazar. In this, as in so many other matters in the years to come, my mother prevailed and upended the long-standing custom of our branch of the Molhos. The first son of the eldest son had to be either

Figure 2.10. *The author, about two years old, not at all ready for the adventures that awaited him.*

Saul or Lazar. My father, eldest son of an eldest son and oldest of seven children, was Saul Molho, son of Lazar, who himself had been the son of Saul Molho. When my turn came, I, eldest son of an eldest son, should have been Lazar Molho, son of Saul, son of Lazar.... But, in a sign that, in the years before the Holocaust, among some Sephardic Jews, friendship could be thicker than blood, the chain of Molho names was broken. It took one of my father's younger brothers, Uncle Isaac, to revive a variant of this family tradition by naming his son, who was born in 1953, Lazar.

I suspect that, when he came to register my birth at the Jewish community, my father felt a degree of embarrassment. I say this because, many years later, in very different circumstances, I faced the sort of reaction about my name that I imagine my father faced in the summer in 1939. It was in February 1981, when I was in Istanbul to seek legal advice about the estate of one of my mother's Salonica-born uncles, who, as I mentioned earlier, had settled in Istanbul shortly after the annexation of Salonica by Greece. Taken by one of my father's cousins (who also had left Salonica to settle in Istanbul shortly after World War I) to the office of one of the city's prominent Jewish lawyers, I was rather unpleasantly greeted: "Why this name," he wanted to know? Saint Anthony "was such a repulsive hermit." *C' est un nom Grec*, he muttered several times throughout our meeting, *ce n' est pas un nom Juif*. Are you sure you were not converted to Christianity? Not even during the war and the German occupation? If not, why couldn't you be a Joseph, or David, or Albert? Since then, I have suspected that he refused to take on my mother's case because he disliked my name. In the eyes of a strictly observant Jew, no Jew could possibly be an Antonios unless he strove to conceal his Jewishness.

Figure 2.11. *With my mother, autumn/winter 1940, in the White Tower Gardens.*

Even so, my parents' decision about my name would have significant consequences for my future. This was especially clear during the Nazi occupation of Greece in the early 1940s. My Greek name made it easier for me to be hidden by a series of families that took me in during the war. There was no need to dissimulate by taking on a different name, a practice of just about every Jew in occupied Greece. My mother went from Lily to Eleni, my father Saul took the name of Savas, my Uncle Isaac and Uncle Raphael became, respectively, Yannis, and Nicos. I was Antonis (or, as Sister Anastasia in the Catholic convent where I was hidden for several months starting in June 1943 called me, Antonakis, a diminutive, and even more Greek sounding name). No sooner had the Germans left than Jews reverted to their authentic pre-1943 names. But I was spared this double change. I remained attached to my one Greek name. Whenever the occasion demanded it, my name let me straddle the world of my Jewish home and the larger Greek universe in which I lived a good part of my daily life.

My earliest memory of my name goes back to late 1942 or early 1943, when Salonica was under Nazi occupation, and two young German officers were billeted in our house. I see myself standing on the back terrace of my maternal grandparents' house, looking over a wall onto a tiled yard next door, where a boy a little older than me is riding a tricycle. It is drizzling. I hear a voice from the house: Tony, *viens dedans. Tout de suite.* Who gave the order? I do not remember. What I do remember is the grayness of the scene. The boy's tricycle. The voice in the back speaking in French. And my name—Tony.

For my family, Antonis had become Tony. But not for everyone. And not for myself, at least not necessarily. If my family would insist on this change, others, outside the family—among the neighborhood gang and, following autumn 1945 when I was first sent to school, my classmates and my teachers—resisted it. In the years immediately before and after the war, "Tony" had a foreign, even perhaps a slightly exotic ring to it. If I could not be Antonis, an invented, uncommon abbreviation of my official name's form, would do. I would be Tonis. Two or three letters of the alphabet can make a whole lot of difference to a young boy. Turn a "y" into an "is"—Tony into Tonis—and the boy gets a different sense of how he fits, or doesn't, into the surrounding world.

There were thousands of Antonises in Salonica after the war. To the best of my knowledge, I was then one of the city's handful of Tonys. Another Tony, who also lived on Evzonon Street, was the concert pianist Tony Georgiou, born in Salonica but, as word had it, of Romanian origin. His piano playing was spellbinding, and I still remember noticeably slowing my pace as I walked by his house at the end of a school day to take in the torrent of notes that floated from his house onto the street. To us, young boys after the war, it did not seem strange that someone as exotic as Mr. Georgiou—Romanian in origin and a classical pianist—would be called Tony.

But how did the name fit the image of a young boy such as myself, always keen to think of himself as normal and to fit in his surroundings? The name was neither fully Greek nor traditionally Jewish nor did it contain the cache of European, mostly French, names carried by some of Salonica's middle-class Jews—Albert, Richard, Maurice, Jacques.... To be sure, an occasional artist—such as, especially following the war, the very popular Tonis Maroudas and the actor Tonis Yakovakis—rendered the name familiar to Greek audiences and reduced somewhat the name's foreign tone to many of my contemporaries. Still, both forms of the name—Tony and Tonis—were unusual, or, as Mrs. Christidou, our neighbor across street, Liolia's mother, once said as we were all sitting at the beach after the war, it was a special name, by which she probably meant that it was unusual and somewhat strange. I have the sense that, in calling me Tony, my parents, especially my mother, intended to somehow set me apart from my classmates and friends. Tony made me into someone who would fit in a distant and only vaguely known place, in America, or, as my staunchly philo-American mother would often correct me, in the United States. If as a Molho I could fit comfortably in Salonica's recognizably Jewish community, and as Antonis into my Greek surroundings, Tony carried me beyond both Jewish and Greek environments. The name made me see myself, precisely because this was the way that I, as the name's bearer, was perceived, as an outsider or, perhaps to be more precise, as someone who was neither entirely Jewish nor entirely Greek, a boy who, as the occasion called for, at times was detached from while at other times fitted into his surroundings.

So, for public functions, in the eyes of the state, school authorities, and some of my teachers, I was Antonis. As for myself, whenever I had to think about these matters, the game was open, even if its rules, and more significantly its results, were not always clear. I would play along, projecting now this, now that persona, never fully aware nor entirely unaware of the consequences.

There is a scrap of evidence I stumbled upon not long ago that makes me think that the preceding are not retrospective fantasies. Yiorgos Christides, Liolia's brother, lived with his family across the street from us, we at 24 Evzonon Street, they at number 21. In the years immediately following the war, he was, by far, my closest friend. We spent hours playing together, running in and out of each other's homes, concocting made-up worlds of pirates, musketeers, and Robin Hoods. For birthdays, we gave each other presents. He, having lived until very recently in the very house where he grew up more than eighty years ago, has kept the presents I gave him. Given my itinerant life, I do not have his. In the course of a visit to his summer home sometime in the 1990s, his pretty, young daughter, nudged on by her father's smilingly conspiratorial wink, showed me a wonderfully illustrated children's book. Did I remember it, she wanted to know? I didn't. Look to the front page, she urged me. There, in my meticulous, childish handwriting I read the inscription I had originally written in English: "To my dearest friend, Giorgi, from Tony—May, 1947." But the "y" in my name had been corrected. It had been "is." Tony had been imposed on Tonis. My mother, who was then in her mid-eighties and present in this encounter, denied remembering anything about the book or about the inscription.

Much later, after I had moved to the United States, I would be given yet another name. Anthony, an anglicized version of Antonios. The translation was an immigration officer's decision of what my American name should have been. Molho sounded vaguely Italian to the officer. Anthony was an appropriate prefix. Squeezed into the officer's cubicle of an office, I was too slow to react and to insist that I already had an American name: Tony. For years before, this had been my imagined American identity. But that was before I had ever set foot in the United States. Now that I had left home and taken the first steps toward settling there, my official name was fixed. For most of my colleagues and acquaintances, in the United States and elsewhere, even in Greece, I became Anthony Molho.

So, a decision taken by my parents when, for a short while, some barriers between Salonica's Christians and Jews had become a little more porous than before, deeply colored my life. Not, of course, that my name fixed my destiny. But it surely served me, mostly well, in varied circumstances, especially during the years of the war and during the German occupation of Greece.

3.
Hide and Seek

The Germans occupied Salonica in April 1941. Mussolini's Italians had invaded Greece in October 1940 but were trounced by an inspired Greek counteroffensive, so Hitler was forced to intervene to settle matters in the southern Balkans. The Wehrmacht swept through the Greek frontier, and within days, the German flag was flying on top of the White Tower, the old Ottoman fort that over the centuries had become the city's trademark, as much as the Parthenon was the trademark of Athens. I was then not quite two and a half years old and have no direct memory of those unhappy days.

Still, almost immediately after the war, I was often shown pictures of the damage caused by Italian air raids to buildings and to the port, not far from my father's and my grandfather's stores. German tanks triumphantly entered the city in April 1941 and were posted in key locations, one of which was very close to where my grandmother lived. All family members were now gathered in my grandmother's apartment at 53 Nikis Boulevard, right on the corniche, and during the air raids, everyone would rush down to the building's basement waiting for the sirens to sound the all-clear. In the first weeks after our return to Salonica, Uncle Roufa with great gusto would recount to me stories about our days when, together with residents of other apartments, we were all squeezed into a small dark basement space. There, by his telling, at least once a day, the first great confrontation between my mother and me took place under the eyes of the entire family. The battle of the pudding, as Uncle Roufa called it, pitted my mother's determination to feed me a pudding that she thought was good for me, and my equal determination to refuse my mother's entreaties to allow her to feed me. No less forceful in small matters than in large, my mother would not abide my resistance. Italian bombs were falling a few blocks away, sirens were blasting, ambulances and fire trucks rushing just outside the apartment, while I was engaged in an epic battle with my mother over my diet. I would keep my mouth tightly shut, resolutely refusing even to taste the silly pudding. Losing her patience, she would finally grab me, lie me flat on my back, and try to squeeze the spoon full of pudding in my mouth. I would stick to my guns, until my resistance gave way when, furious at me, my mother would close my nose so that, instinctively, I would open my mouth to breathe. Just at that moment, despite my cries and tears, my mouth would be filled with a spoonful of pudding. No matter the protests of uncles and grandmother that this was no way to feed a little two-year-old boy, the violent confrontation would continue to the last spoonful. At that point, it seems that my father would make his presence felt by telling my mother that the scene should not be repeated. But by my uncle's telling, the battle would promptly resume at the next meal. Ironically, one of the books I remember seeing in our house as I was growing up was Dr. Spock's manual, *Baby and Child Care*, that had gained some popularity among middle-class mothers in Salonica after the war. I can't imagine what my mother found in it that was appealing to her, given her instinctively disciplinarian penchant as regards child rearing.

These are the sort of memories, implanted in me, that have survived in my mind from the years between the Germans' arrival in the city and spring 1943. By late spring 1941, with the German presence stabilized in Greece, we returned home, to be with my other grandparents, who had continued to live with their other daughter *Tante* Marcella and *Oncle* Richard in their family home. A couple of incidents, perhaps because of their strangeness, have stuck with me from those years. One of our neighbors on Evzonon Street was a young man—he was almost certainly Jewish—who had been conscripted and come back from the Albanian front. Like many Greek soldiers sent to fight in the mountains ill clad and ill equipped, he returned home with very bad frost bite and had to have a leg amputated. The story of his heroism and of his sad fate had been recounted to me by someone in the family, and one day I was taken to visit him at his house, which was directly next door to ours. I think I was sent there accompanied by one of our maids, who left me alone in the wounded hero's room. It was, I think, in late 1942 or very early 1943.

I still have a vague memory of myself perched at the foot of his bed. I did not know what to say. Probably, he was as much at a loss for words as I was. But to make me feel better, he explained that soon he would start improving because, with time, his leg would grow back in place. His account left a very deep impression on me. If his leg could grow back in place, why could not something similar also happen to me? Later that day, having returned home, I made my way to the kitchen where my grandmother found me with a large knife in hand struggling to cut my neck. The story made the rounds in the family and was repeated

COURAGE AND COMPASSION

after the war. It seems, I had explained to my grandmother, that I wanted to put to a test the wounded soldier's tale and see if my head might grow again once I succeeded in cutting it off! Everyone in the family was struck by what they took to be my cleverness, save for my grandfather who wondered out loud to anyone willing to listen to him about how it was possible for him to have such a dumb grandson. That was my first brush with war. I would come close to it a few more times later, although I cannot claim that during those years I would feel the fear that war engenders in people. Still, I learned from my wounded neighbor that war does have consequences. If only nature were as generous with the wounded as the young amputee had tried to make me believe! After the war, I was told that the young man had been carried off to Auschwitz where he was murdered.

Then there is the case of the two young German soldiers who, for a period of a few months (or was it only weeks?) were billeted in our house. I wish I knew their names. What was their background? What did they think of having to stay (or being ordered to stay) in the home of a Jewish family? Even more so, I wish I could find out their fates. Did they survive the war, or did they perish somewhere in the Balkans or on the Russian front, as so many young German and Russian men did before the war's end? Might they have been killed a little later by an action of the Greek underground, which my father joined in the summer of 1943? Their presence in our house strikes me now as odd, almost irreconcilable with the images of the German occupation of Salonica I had nurtured over many years after the war. A few people outside Greece, to whom I recounted this story, also thought it was very unusual for German soldiers to be billeted in a Jewish home. Obviously, I do not remember them well at all, except for a faded image that has lingered on in my mind: tall, uniformed young men, whose blondness struck me as strange. I was not quite four years old, but their presence has remained alive in my mind for more than three-quarters of a century. In my imagination over all those years since the war, these two young men did not fit the image of German soldiers whom most Greeks—Jews and Christians—have thought of as being impersonations of evil. Their actions made them appear (because perhaps they were) deeply human, people who tried to alleviate hardships caused by themselves and their superiors. These two young men behaved in ways that have struck me (and also struck my once intensely anti-German mother) as peculiar. At some point soon after their arrival in our house they were told, probably by my father who was fluent in German, that my maternal grandfather with whom we were then living, suffered from heart problems and that his doctor (Dr. Vaïnanidis, the one whose name I had been given) had recommended that there not be any commotion or much noise in the house. The family's plea was met, and these two young men soon began to take off their heavy boots each day when returning home and leave them in the corridor in front of our apartment so as not to make noise while walking in the house. And then, when they discovered that our family had difficulty finding in the black market medicines that my grandfather badly needed, they would on occasion return home with the medicines in question, procured by them, who knows how or where. In fact, one of the two took the habit, when he returned at home in the evenings, to pay a call to my bed-ridden grandfather to chitchat about this and that. My mother thought that they spoke in French but was unsure of that. Based on what my mother told me years later, my parents had come to trust these two young men. When, once, they had to attend a funeral and did not want to leave me with my grandparents so as not to disturb them, they asked one of these soldiers to babysit me. Just think of it, I had a Nazi soldier as a babysitter! It is the stuff of which a Borges story might have been written. Then, one day, they appeared at the house, gathered their belongings and left. They gave no explanation save that they had been given orders to leave the house. Their presence in our house was like an apparition. They came, they helped, and they left.

But the memory of their existence lingered on, offering a minor counterpoint to what was about to happen. Decades later, while I was living in Rhode Island, my wife and I invited to our home a newly arrived colleague, V. B., his wife, and three children to share our Thanksgiving dinner with us. They were German, about my age, and, over the years, they became close friends. My mother, then in her mid-seventies, happened to have been visiting us for the holiday. My wife and I rather hesitantly mentioned to her that we would have dinner guests, and that they were German. She said nothing, but her sour face gave away her displeasure. The dinner went extremely well, our guests were wonderfully sociable and extremely courteous to my mother. That evening, as we were cleaning up after our guests had left, my mother mentioned sheepishly that these were wonderful people, unlike other Germans. They reminded her, she added, of the two German officers billeted in our house during the German occupation. Good actions do have a way of making an impression. Perhaps not always, but often enough to soften hard positions formed in the midst of unusually dangerous times, which left bitter memories on those who experienced them.

Indeed, there was no question at all that those were hard times. In the first two years of occupation, for all the important adjustments, life continued with a semblance of order. By the beginning of 1943, things began taking a very much more ominous turn. The Nazi regime made its intentions ever clearer, and uncertainties and anxiety among Salonican Jews increased sharply. What was in store for the future? How could one seek to safeguard families and friends? By then, possibilities of escape did not exist. In any case, where could one flee? To escape, you had to know someone, willing to take you in, and this someone had to live in a country that could be reached relatively easily. For us, the options were limited. Istanbul, where my mother's uncle and my father's aunt and her family had settled in the late 1910s was inaccessible: Turkey did not allow refugees to cross its borders. Traveling to Cairo, where, together with the Greek government-in-exile, one of my father's brothers had taken flight in 1941, was impossible due to the war. Conakry, in French Guinea, where another of my father's brothers had settled earlier, was very distant, and travel to it would have required crossing French colonial territories, now themselves at war. And because of British policy, Palestine was largely inaccessible to Jews. In any case, my grandfather's health made any plan of escape for the entire family unrealistic. Everyone was now terrorized about the future. What was in store for us Jews when the Germans began circulating news about the imminent resettlement of the entire Jewish community to new homes in faraway Poland?

In mid-March (1943), my parents put into action a plan they must have pondered for a while. By then, it was clear that the Germans were serious about their plans to rid Salonica of Jews. The first step in implementing this design was the creation of a ghetto, the first ever in Salonica's history. Jews were forced to move into a designated area in town, while access into or out of it was controlled. This was the part of town to the east of the White

Tower, which, fortunately for us, included our house. Then, step by step, Germans began unfolding their ultimate intentions. On 15 March, the first train convoys brimming with local Jews left, carrying their human cargo to Poland. No one knew exactly what was going on, but the signs were not encouraging.

At that point, my parents decided that they would protect me by giving me away to a Christian family. Only after the war, when my mother impulsively recounted the story to anyone willing to listen to her, did I learn the details of these heart-rending discussions and of the false starts that led to my removal from our family home. It turns out that *Oncle* Richard, my mother's older brother, who was well connected in town, tended to the logistics of this operation. He spoke with friends, trying to entice them to overlook the risk of sheltering a Jewish boy with the promise that, if for some reason my parents did not survive the war, they could raise me as their own. In the next three or so months, I lived in succession with two childless, middle-aged couples.

So, on a fateful day, I found myself in the home of two unknown people, whose names I do not now remember. I must have stayed with them only for a few days, a week at most. Later, I was told that they soon got cold feet because of the risk of keeping me and pressed my parents to take me back. I have no recollection at all of my arrival at their house. Who took me there? What did my parents tell me about what I could expect? How did I react? I do not remember. But I do have a vague memory of my hosts (given the brevity of my stay with them, I could hardly call them surrogate parents) as tall, and formal people, who lived in a commodious apartment—at least that's how they appeared to my eyes. To a not quite four-year-old boy, two middle-aged strangers might in any case appear to be tall and formal. I do not remember their showing me any affection or tenderness. What has stuck in my mind is an unusual episode that probably took place the day of my arrival.

The three of us are sitting in the dining room, furnished with imposingly heavy furniture. I think I remember a big vase full of flowers standing on the buffet. A woman, she was probably the maid, wearing a blue apron, enters from the kitchen, carrying a bowl of steaming soup. The lady of the house takes the bowl, serves her husband and herself, and carefully places the bowl on the table. They start eating, while, simultaneously, carrying on an intense conversation. I sit there befuddled. No one is paying attention to me. Worse, there is nothing on my plate. I wonder: What will I eat? Why don't they serve me? Why do they completely ignore me? Should I ask to be served? I distinctly remember thinking: Perhaps they are putting me to a test. They want to see if I am a well-behaved boy and can patiently wait my turn. Or else they are punishing me for my behavior—although, I keep telling myself, I have done nothing wrong. My mother must have told me to be well behaved and to cause no trouble. I sit politely until abruptly the lady takes stock of me. I think she spoke in French but I can't quite remember. My God! She exclaims. We forgot the child. A bowl of soup very soon appears under my nose, and this strange memory ends here. A few days later, I was taken back home to my parents.

Following my return, the search for another refuge continued, with my uncle, once again, coming up with a possibility. Another friendly couple were disposed—indeed, eager—to have me. It seems that they made solemn, impassioned promises to my parents. They would look after me as if I were their own child. My parents should have no concern for my wellbeing. After the war, I was told that they had been paid something to cover the extra costs of my presence in their home—I have no idea how much. Whatever the sum, it would have been inadequate to cover their risk or their affection and care for me. So, as my mother later told me, late one night, I was bundled up and carried over to their house, which was outside the ghetto, very near the cinema Ilissia, a stone's throw from the White Tower. For the next two or more months I lived with *Mamà* Elpida (Mother Hope), and *Babàs* Yiorgos. By the time I left their home on my adventurous trip to join my parents in Athens, I had become more than casually attached to them. They were gentle, indeed affectionate, with me and tried to spoil me and make me forget the trauma of my separation from home. I do not think they were well-to-do. They lived in a semi-basement flat, modestly but not uncomfortably furnished.

I know that, if I had been orphaned during the war, they would have been good and supportive guardians. The messages I scribbled down to them during the war, after I joined my mother in Athens, more like scrawls and doodles typical of a five-year-old, expressed my affection for them in the period immediately after my departure from their house. In all truth, these two individuals had acted as surrogate parents for me, all the while exposing themselves to considerable risk. If they were caught, they would have been harshly punished. I also know that, in case neither my father nor mother survived the occupation, the family strategy was that, after the war, I would have been taken care by one of my father's four brothers; since two of them lived in Africa, one in Cairo, the other in Conakry, there was a good chance that, if I was lucky enough to survive, I would most probably have ended up in a Molho household.

I think there is something curious about my memories. Some parts are deeply ingrained in my mind. I remember the corner of the sitting room (a sort of alcove) where a small cot had been set up for me. I remember my anxiety about sleeping alone in that cot, and Elpida's (but not her husband's) eagerness to have me tuck in with them at night, so that I could be cosseted in their bed's comforting warmth. I also remember the tin cup that was given me, from which to drink my milk in the morning. And perhaps obviously, I remember sitting on the floor of the sitting room, playing for stretches of time with my toys that someone had brought to my new house from my old one. But there are points on which my memory has failed me. I do not remember being cold in that house. Nor do I remember any smells, which I should because the kitchen was just abutting the large room where we spent most of our time. And I do not remember at all what we ate. I assume that I had been well fed because, when a couple of months later I arrived in Athens, by my mother's later recollection, I was still chubby and obviously well taken care of. Yet, there is one important detail that has completely disappeared from my memory: what did Elpida and Yiorgos look like? I simply have no recollection of their physical appearance. I find this gap in my memory disturbing. Why should there be this sort of lacuna in my mind, when I know—because I remember—the kindness and warmth that they expressed toward me, my affection for them even after my departure from their house, the not infrequent references to them in my conversations with my mother following my having joined my parents in Athens a little more than two months after my arrival at Yiorgos and Elpida's house? In later years, my mother and sister, not to speak of my wives—all three of them—often teased me for not remembering details of their appearance, what color dress did they wear a few hours or days earlier, did they have long or short hair, had they pinned a simple or colorful broach on their overcoat? My inability to fasten my attention onto this sort of detail may also account for my failure to remember details of Elpida's and Yiorgos's appearance.

Even so, my gratitude to them should be boundless. Yet, an incident in the summer or autumn of 1945, shortly after the end of the war, complicated my feelings about my stay at their house. By then, following a two-year absence, we had returned to Salonica, retaken possession of our old house, and tried, in the heavy atmosphere of those months, to resume the semblance of a regular life. One afternoon my parents took me along to visit Elpida and Yiorgos at the house where I had spent more than two months in the spring of 1943, a little more than two years earlier. I suppose the purpose of this social call was to thank them for taking care of me and to give me a chance to become reacquainted with them. But something went astray in this visit, and I think it was the last time I saw Yiorgos and Elpida. We sat in the living room, vaguely familiar surroundings to me, and I recall pointing to my parents features of the house that I still remembered. The adults' conversation was intense, my mother more than once emotionally recalling the deportations to Auschwitz of her brother Richard, sister, and parents. I remember that *Mamà* Elpida (as I continued to call her) repeatedly hugged and kissed me, and *Babàs* Yiorgos sat me on his lap and teased and tickled me. But shortly before our departure, the tone of our encounter changed. At a certain point, both our hosts left the room, and my mother, pointedly although in a soft voice, asked my father if he recognized a pair of yellow and white curtains on the windows. Of course he did, they were from a bolt of cloth that had been left in our house when we left. Nothing had been mentioned as to how that cloth had found its way to this other house, and why Elpida and Yiorgos would have used it without asking or even acknowledging its presence to my parents. I distinctly remember my mother shaking her head, a dark expression marking her face.

I do not remember ever hearing again anything else about that bolt of cloth. But I think I understand my mother's bitterness. It is perhaps important to remember the atmosphere that prevailed in Salonica in the months following the deportation of the Jews to Poland. Hundreds of apartments, nearly all of them with all their contents and perhaps as large a number of stores—sometimes important businesses—were abandoned to their fate. Dozens of Christian families simply stepped in, often with the consent of the occupying authorities, and appropriated these properties. A culture of theft—it is hardly possible for me to think about what happened in terms other than thievery—prevailed in the city, with the collaborationist authorities offering cover for the aggressive appropriations of those months. All too many times after the war, neighbors and acquaintances explained that objects—some of considerable value, others, such as merchandise from my father's store, still others, mementos or small objects of little material value—had disappeared unaccountably from their homes or stores, or that warehouses where my father had tried to hide them had been burglarized. I have a letter written during the war and addressed to my father but sent to his brother Isaac, and signed by N., who in an unctuous and apologetic tone explained that all the goods left in his custody by my father had simply vanished from his warehouse. After the war, N. presented himself as a family friend, someone concerned with our well-being, who had done everything he could to protect us and our property. Neither of my parents believed him or much cared to see him, although, on a few occasions, circumstances forced us to socialize with him and his family. In this context, a pair of curtains removed from our house is a trifle one should not exaggerate. Yet, in my parents' view that pair of curtains had come to stand for the unspeakable injustices and intolerable behavior of many of our neighbors and acquaintances.

To be sure, this is not the whole story. Shortly before my grandparents' deportation, a small safety deposit box with my grandmother's and the family jewels was entrusted for safekeeping to Dr. Vaïnanidis. No sooner had we returned home, in spring 1945, he brought it home to us. What I remember about his visit was not my mother's exclamation that the box had not even been opened during our absence. Rather, what I vividly recall, is Dr. Vaïnanidis arriving at our home in his horse drawn gig, and his asking me to hold the horse's reins while he descended holding a box that had no particular meaning for me. I can still see some of these jewels in the picture I mentioned earlier, of my grandmother posing with her husband, her son, and her daughter (my mother) around 1918 or 1919. Long after the war, some rings and a couple of necklaces she wore in that picture eventually found their way to my sister and to my daughters.

But there is more. Today, in one of the long corridors of my house, I have hung a number of family photographs dating from before the war: a picture of my mother with her classmates when she was in kindergarten or first grade, her face, already then, marked by a determined look, so similar to my sister's when she was that age; my parents' wedding picture; my mother and I posing before a camera in the gardens surrounding the White Tower when I was a little more than one year old; the formal portraits of my maternal grandparents; my father and his classmates' graduation picture from the French lycée, ca. 1916 or 1917; a picture of my mother's beautiful sister Marcella (who died in Auschwitz and for whom my sister, born in 1946,

Figure 3.1. *My mother, standing in front row, the last one on the right, with her classmates at the Lycée Français, 1919–20.*

was named); and several more. Whenever friends ask me about these pictures, it pleases me to recount how many of them were returned to us after the war. It turns out that when, in stages, we were forced to flee our house from late March to early April 1943, many of the pictures that hang on my corridor walls were placed in a large, red cardboard box and left in a cupboard. Someone who shortly thereafter occupied our apartment threw this red box in the street. There the box with its precious contents lay for a while (perhaps only for an hour or two), until our next-door neighbor, the soft-spoken Dr. Pestelmatzian, an Armenian doctor, a refugee who fled with his family from the Ottoman Empire following the persecution of Armenians there, picked them up, kept them for the duration of the war, and returned them to us when we returned home.

Figure 3.2. *My father's graduation, perhaps in 1916, from the (French?) school. My father, standing, last on the right. His brother, my Uncle Isaac, sitting, second from left.*

Figure 3.3. *Aunt Marcella, my mother's younger sister. Murdered in Auschwitz. Photo perhaps taken at the time of her engagement to Pepo Carasso, early 1940s.*

I have often wondered why he had taken the trouble to collect and keep this box. No doubt, he was a kind and sensitive person—that might be sufficient as an explanation. Yet, I have also wondered if there might be something more to it. Might his kindness also express a sense of solidarity of someone whose community had been subjected to terrible persecution only a few decades earlier, and who could, in his own imagination, understand our suffering? The memory of his and other Armenians' persecution and their forced flight from their homes a generation or two earlier may have sharpened his sensibility to the worth of such objects, of no value to anyone other than the people immediately concerned. I should have asked him or his two daughters, who were about a dozen years older than me, why they had taken the trouble to save a storehouse of someone else's family memories. I never knew him well enough to ask, and, frankly, questions such as this did not cross my mind then.

In recent years, the yellow curtains and the pictures in the red cardboard box have intrigued me. Why have these family belongings continued to hold such a fascination for me? Perhaps what I find intriguing about them is the different path each followed during and after the war and the symbolism each holds for me. The curtains have come to stand in my mind for the distance between my family and Salonica's dominant Orthodox society. As I was thinking out loud about this with a friend, he responded that of course the curtains had been stolen from us, as had so much else. And, as this friend (who, significantly, is German) added, what is important in this incident is that these objects were not stolen by German soldiers but by Greeks. On the surface of it, this friend continued, they had been friendly to you and your family, but it seems, without a second thought, they considered it natural to remove from our house (or to put it another way, perhaps exaggerating only slightly, to steal) an object belonging to a friendly Jewish family and to exhibit it without hesitation in their home. To make things more complex, as I already mentioned, they had run an unusual risk to shelter me. The pictures, and their circuitous return to our family, evoke altogether something else. They are witnesses to the solidarity of a neighborly family. Perhaps also they indicate that a sense of community did exist in our street and that we, the Molhos and Alkalays of Evzonon Street, were part of that community.

A day after my arrival in my new home with *Babàs* Yiorgos and *Mamà* Elpida an incident occurred that has stayed with me ever since. For years, until well into my twenties, my recurring nightmares were related to this scene. Since then, I have had few nightmares, but they have all been centered on my possible abandonment. What I remember is this: I am sleeping deeply in a dark room, when, abruptly, I open my eyes and see my father, bending over me. Later, I was told that he had come to see me one more time, hours before he, two of his brothers, my mother, and two close friends were to set off from Salonica in an attempt to escape. In my memory, my father has just kissed me and is softly stepping back so as not to wake me. But, startled, I do wake up, and, in the semidarkness, I discern his shadow. I throw my arms in the air, imploring him to pick me up from my small bed. Simultaneously, I let out a scream that reverberated in my head for years. Someone turns on the light, and a pair of arms gently lift me from my bed. The memory ends there.

Had I been frightened because of the brusque awakening? Did the sight of my father, a few days after my second removal from our house, release the fear and uncertainty—but also the longing for home—that must have followed me in the preceding days? I do not remember crying again during the war. And for many years thereafter, I cried very little: not when, after the war, I was the recipient of a healthy spanking by my disciplinarian mother, nor when I would fall and hurt myself, nor even when I attended funerals, even of people who had been dear to me. That night's scream seems to have purged me, in ways that I cannot even begin to fathom, of my urge to cry. It took me years to regain the gift of crying. Perhaps I did so, at last, when I was able to face up to these memories and be partly released from the burden of fears and complexes deeply buried in me during the course of my wartime adventures.

A conversation shortly after the war has stayed in my mind. I was about six or seven, and for reasons that I do not now remember, the discussion with my mother turned on my stay with Elpida and Yiorgos. For all the resentment triggered by the disappearance of the bale of cloth (and, it turns out, of many other objects), my mother continued to feel deeply indebted to my two caretakers. They had taken good care of me and kept me safe from the ever-vigilant eyes of the Nazi occupiers and their local collaborators, always eager to collect the rewards promised to anyone who turned in Jews—children or adults. It would have been easy to spot a new and sudden arrival in the neighborhood, especially a young boy whose family ties with his hosts could not be easily explained. Of course, I was mostly unaware of all that, although I have the sense that something inside me, a sort of reflexive defensiveness, made me more cautious than I had been before, leading me to be more alert to dangers around me. I have no evidence to support this claim, although it is unquestionable that I grew to be more cautious, less impetuous than I had been at home. But was I really more alert to dangers around me? Only slowly after the war, listening to the adults recount, over and over again, the details of these seemingly surreal stories did the reality of the situation sink in. Before that, it seems like I was somnambulating, groping in the half dark, only half aware of the world I was living in.

On the occasion of that conversation and of several others, my mother pressed me to talk to her about my routine while I was living with my surrogate parents: how did I spend my hours every day, what did I do to keep myself occupied, with whom did I play in the street near the house, who visited us at home during my stay there? My responses to her questions were simple and straightforward: I had not played with any children, not met much of anyone, as I did not remember visitors coming to the house, nor did I recall visiting parks or nearby squares. On one occasion, I do remember being taken by Yiorgos to a café, where I sat with him for a while. My grandfather's house, where my mother had grown up, and where, eventually, my parents had settled following their marriage, was large and commodious. Our apartment in it had two large balconies and a very large garden where I had freely roamed under our gardener's supervision. Elpida and Yiorgos's house, essentially a small and somewhat dark apartment, provided few of these amenities. There was not much to do in the house, although I recall that some of my old toys miraculously appeared in my new home, having been deposited in the sitting room either by my new or old parents. I recall spending hours sitting on the floor playing with those toys. I suspect that this isolation and the lack of a chance to play with other children rather left its mark on me. Essentially, I spent those more than two months indoors, alone, except for the company of my new parents.

I do not remember the circumstances of my leaving *Mamà* Elpida and *Babàs* Yiorgos. My parents left Salonica late in the evening of the day following my arrival in my new home. Their trip to Athens was adventurous, almost beyond belief. In her oral testimony about her wartime experiences, my mother described the movie-like details of my parents' escape from German-occupied Greece to the temporary safety of the Italian-occupied part of the country. From there, they wrote to my caretakers in Salonica to inquire about my condition. But soon a dispute arose with them. Elpida and Yiorgos wanted to adopt me right away. My parents did not consent, and, fearing that I would either be baptized against their will or that false papers would be produced to show that I was my custodians' biological child, they demanded that I be returned to them. By then, my grandparents, together with my Aunt Marcella (my mother's younger sister) and her new husband, Pepo Carasso, had been betrayed to the Germans it seems by one of the two notorious Hasson brothers, local Jews who had collaborated with the Germans, and would soon be carried to their death in Auschwitz. For his part, *Oncle* Richard had also been sent to Auschwitz. Someone else, I am not sure who, mediated to arrange for my removal to Athens, where my parents had, in the meantime, found hiding places. From there they would try to make more long-term arrangements for the future.

A plan had to be concocted to transport me from Salonica to Athens. My father knew someone who worked as an engineer in the state railways, and he was entrusted with the task of delivering me to Athens. In this instance also a payment was made, but however large it may have been it was inadequate to cover the risk of accompanying me on my trip. The trip must have lasted more than one day, perhaps as much as two or three days, with only a few details surviving in my mind. But I do have a vague memory of long stops, when we waited who knows for what, when I was not allowed to climb down from the engine room. I do also remember being given small chunks of cheese and bread to eat. The engineer who took it upon himself to accompany me to my parents was all too aware that he ran a big risk for shielding a Jewish boy. The train trip from Salonica to Athens was made even more dangerous by the fact that, while Salonica and most of northern Greece were under German occupation, the area south of Lamia, with the exception of Athens, was occupied by Italian forces. Thus, somewhere around the town of Lamia, a border had to be crossed with papers checked by the German and Italian authorities, assisted by their Greek collaborators.

I do recall some details of this adventurous escape. Some other details were recounted to me immediately after the war by the engineer himself, in one of his periodic visits to my father's store. My father's friend had been unable to procure false papers for me but was disposed to fabricate a story to conceal my identity. Busybodies who asked about me would be told that I, Antonakis, was his nephew—his sister having recently moved to Athens to find work, had left me in his care—and he was now bringing me to my mother. Folks who asked might have been satisfied with this story. But facing authorities was a different matter. Germans and their Greek minions might not have accepted this explanation and would have tried to see if I was circumcised. Thus, the engineer decided that at the time of the border crossing I would have to hide in some corner where soldiers and police were unlikely to poke around.

But where? My guardian had arranged to be in sole charge of the engine room, where he and I were the only occupants. Most of the space in that room was taken up by two immense boilers, placed next to each other. The one to the right, next to the door through which one climbed into the engine room, was in operation. I recall the engineer every now and then stoking this boiler with coal. But the boiler on the left (further away from the entrance) was not being used. In fact, it was empty. I suspect this particular engine was chosen for the trip, so that the empty boiler could serve as a convenient hiding place for me. At some point, I was told to climb into the empty boiler and warned to be absolutely quiet. After the war, as he recounted this part of the story, the engineer remembered having told me not to make a peep. I listened to his instructions and dutifully climbed in and accommodated myself in the boiler. I do not remember what happened next. Perhaps, as was often the case in later years whenever I was inactive and bored for a long time, I simply fell asleep. I do not remember if the border guards climbed in the engine room, if the engineer had a discussion with them, or at what point I was asked to climb out of the boiler.

My next memory is of the train arriving in the Athens train station. I climbed down the iron steps out of the engine room following my guardian who took me by the hand and led me to a green field that I remember distinctly. In the distance, I saw my parents and one of my father's brothers, *Oncle* Isaac, who by then had become Uncle Yannis. I rushed to them, fell in my mother's open arms and blurted out what Yiorgos and Elpida had instructed me to tell them: They have taken away grandpapa and grandmaman. I had no idea what that meant. But, like a good boy, I discharged my mission.

4.

Fuga or the Long March

The morning after the night of 21 March 1943, assuming that I was in safe hands, my parents put the next step of the plan into action. Speed was essential, and the plan complex. First, a secure home had to be found for my paternal grandmother, Flora, who, at the age of almost seventy, was not in condition to participate in adventurous escapes. By then, she was a widow, and her only support came from her five sons who were still alive. In her case, we were fortunate. Maurice (Uncle Moussa to his friends and relatives) was living thousands of miles away in Conakry, French Guinea in Africa, but his Christian wife, my Aunt Kety, provided the key to finding shelter for my grandmother. Thanks to her family connections who hailed from Kozani, Mrs. Katina was found. I am ashamed to say I do not remember her last name. She was alone (she was a widow or perhaps a spinster) and lived in a small house, little more than a shack, near Salonica. I remember this house, because, in a sort of pilgrimage to my grandmother's wartime refuge, my parents took me there shortly after the war. I also remember her being a tiny woman, always dressed in black, serious but never in bad humor. I am unsure exactly what arrangements were made with Mrs. Katina by my father and his two brothers who were in Salonica. A few gold sovereigns did change hands, but it would be misleading and grossly unfair to find an explanation for Katina's behavior in this financial incentive. The gold coins helped to cover costs. Her decision to hide my grandmother in her house was an expression of her character and of her values: when you see somebody in mortal danger, you help, even if your altruism exposes you to risk your life. For years after the war, thanks to her generosity and willingness to take uncommon risk, she received a monthly allowance from her wartime guest's sons and was able to live in a nice small apartment in Salonica's center, not far from my grandmother's house. Naturally, my grandmother was immensely grateful to her; she always insisted on inviting Katina for lunch, and I remember the big hugs they exchanged whenever they met.

One detail of my grandmother's stay with Katina may be worth recounting. Every time the two met in my presence, my grandmother would repeat it to me. In one of the periodic raids to their neighborhood, German soldiers barged into Katina's house and demanded to know who the toothless old hag lying in a small bed shivering under the blankets was. Katina explained that she was an old aunt from the countryside who had lost her mind because of war privations, and that, to boot, she was deaf and could hardly speak. They believed the story and left my grandmother untouched. Fortunately. Grandmother Flora's command of Greek was at best approximate (after all, she had been born in 1876, subject of the Ottoman Empire and had lived nearly all her life in the golden age of Salonica's Jewry, with Ladino, and bits of Hebrew and Turkish for her languages); she had learned some Greek after 1912, but, to the very end, she spoke it with the characteristic lilting accent of Sephardic Jews. Not a chance she could have passed muster if she had been forced to speak or if, in a moment of panic, she had blurted out some innocent-sounding sentences. Here was a case where good luck, a convincing act of dissimulation, the courage of an aged woman, willing to protect a persecuted Jewess whom she had not known until a few weeks before, offered an example of solidarity and kindness that transcended religious or ethnic boundaries.

The day after my parents ensured that I and my grandmother were in reasonably safe hands, they put into action the second part of their plan. The idea was that they would escape from Salonica, accompanied by two of my father's bachelor brothers and two other close friends. All in all, there would be six of them, five men and one woman. Another small band of Jewish acquaintances, about half a dozen of them, also joined the Molho group, determined to make a run for it, and reach, in any way they could, the greater safety of Athens. Initially, the idea was that my mother would stay behind, both to be close to her parents and to watch after me, if only from a distance. But then she changed her mind and asked to go along. My father's insistence and his brother Raphael's (Roufa to friends and family) prevailed over the objections of some members of the group. Let her come, and if she can't make it, we'll find a way to patch things up. It was not a very convincing argument, but the enterprise itself was not altogether convincing, so it was agreed that twenty-eight-year-old Lily would be allowed to go along. What was unknown to all except to my mother, and perhaps my father, was that at the time she was a few weeks pregnant. Had she revealed her condition to the rest, they almost certainly would have left her behind.

The idea was to find a venal German soldier, willing to take a risk for a considerable payment, to drive them at least as far away as the vicinity of Làrissa, on the southern foothills of Mount Olympus. From there, somehow, they would aim for Athens. Their courage and determination to survive were striking. So was their naivety. But in this sort of poker game, naivety and determination were stronger and more valuable cards than caution. All of them hoped that their long-standing habit of mountain hiking (a hobby my father and his brothers had introduced to my mother) would help them get through the rigors of walking a long distance (Salonica is about 500 kilometers from Athens), remain undetected while crossing long stretches of wild countryside, and somehow get themselves from the German-held to the Italian-held part of Greece. The question of what to take from home did not even come up. A small knapsack with a change of clothes would do. No mementos, no photographs, no heavy clothes. If you wanted to survive you could not be burdened down with clutter. Of course, the moment's emotional intensity was great. Yet, they did not lose sight of their goal to escape the brutality of the fate they would inevitably face, and of the risks they would encounter. It would otherwise be difficult to understand their action. Just a few days earlier the first two train convoys carrying Jews to Poland had left Salonica. The Germans' intention to exterminate the city's Jews could hardly have been imagined. Yet, the group acted as if they knew what was at stake for them and their families. Aware of the traps ahead, my father had liquidated many assets, converted them to gold sovereigns, the only currency he was certain they could spend along the way, and tucked these away in his clothes and his knapsack.

Ironically, in the panic at the moment of departure, my mother forgot to change shoes and left wearing her regular city shoes, the hiking boots left in a corner of her parents' living room. But she did not forget to sew two golden sovereigns in each of her stockings—a sort of insurance for the road—although these sovereigns, which she kept in place throughout the war period, did get her in trouble several months later in Athens. In the meantime, an Armenian acquaintance with dealings in town had found a German soldier willing to go along with the scheme. He would "borrow" a German military truck and drive the band of escapees himself. A hefty price in gold sovereigns was agreed upon as was a meeting time and place.

For years after the war, my mother recalled her emotional adieus from her parents. Her father placed his right hand on her head and blessed her, while her mother wept throughout this last encounter, asking out loud what would happen to them now that Lily would not be there to protect them. The two groups met the German driver at Evzonon Street, very close to our home, at about midnight. The payment was made—the German had insisted on full payment in advance—the passengers climbed into the truck, and they left. And so, the flight to safety began. Twelve desperate Jews, at the mercy of a corrupt German soldier. To think or read about it so many years later, it all seems like the script of an extravagantly conceived movie. Yet, by all accounts, this is what happened. My mother's recounting was corroborated time and again by the retelling of the story by all partners in this adventure. Anxiety and fear, relief, exasperation to be leaving home and relatives behind, hope that things would somehow work out, and a general numbness overtook the group.

I suspect that however distraught all of them were, my father must have had the most complex and contradictory feelings. In his youth, he had been a devoted Germanophile, had served as voluntary (unpaid) assistant in the Chair of German literature at the newly founded University of Thessaloniki, had been known to travel on a whim to Vienna to attend opera performances, and prided himself for the German classics, many of them printed in Gothic script, he had collected over the years. Yet, here he was, together with his wife and his brothers, at the mercy of an uncouth German soldier, who, thanks to a handsome payment, had offered to help them evade German control, but who, no doubt, for an equal or greater payment, would not have hesitated a moment to hand them to the authorities. In the middle of the night, as the truck bumped along pitch-black back roads, no one dared to say anything, everyone absorbed in their own thoughts.

But a few kilometers outside Salonica—they had not yet reached Katerini—the truck stopped and, thanks to my mother's telling of the story, I learned my first word of German. *Raus!* shouted the driver. Everybody down. Too dangerous to go any further. The stunned members of the sad cargo climbed down protesting. This was not the agreement. They had paid to be dropped off much further south. Nothing to do. No matter how much the passengers pleaded, the driver was unmoved. At best, he would drive them back to where he had picked them up. Everyone was in despair. The Molho group decided to risk it. The others chose to return. Recently, I learned that, following their return to Salonica, they had their own adventure, escaping first to Epirus, the mountainous region of northwest Greece, from there walking into Albania where they knew some people, who helped them hire a leaky boat to southern Italy, and, finally, on to Egypt, where they spent the war years. After the war they also returned to Salonica. There is a moral to their story, and, of course, also to ours. To have a chance to escape the madness of the Germans you had to move. Staying put in one place was equivalent to signing your own death sentence. This is obvious now, in retrospect. It may have been vaguely clear to some of Salonica's Jews even then. As I think about this episode, I am struck by the fact that for years, until perhaps the 1980s, in my mother's mind, the image of the two polite German soldiers billeted in our house was entirely overshadowed by that of the truck driver who was not only a German but a corrupt one at that.

By my mother's telling, it took them about three weeks to reach Làrissa. The distance was not great, a little less than 150 kilometers, but the roads were unsafe and crossing Mount Olympus was a challenge whose magnitude they had not quite imagined. The unpredictability of their journey, the recurrent fear, which, however, never degenerated into panic, their encounters with mostly helpful peasants and government clerks, but also with some decidedly menacing and unpleasant people, the occasional coup de théâtre that extricated them from what appeared to be a desperate situation—these were the refrains of my mother's stories. Their courage and persistence—and perhaps their despair—helped them make it through. But a not inconsiderable amount of good luck accompanied their daring, and there is no doubt that at least on one occasion my mother's recklessness borne of desperation saved her.

Before continuing this retelling, I should make one point clear. As I already mentioned, I am now recording retellings of stories I heard from my mother, and on occasion from my two uncles, as she was recalling the events she lived through. Rather than trying to reconstruct the details of my mother's recollections, I decided to compress the chronicle of these events and distill them into a few incidents that because of the impression they made on me when I heard them, have remained in my mind, having become, when I was a small boy, transmuted into memories of my own.

As the truck pulled away, the darkness that engulfed the uninviting terrain disoriented the travelers. They trudged along for a short while. While they were walking under a bridge, the sounds of a German patrol made them freeze until the danger passed. Then, the two youngest members of the group—my mother and Uncle Roufa—decided to explore the surroundings, leaving the others under the bridge. Stumbling along in a field, the two explorers spotted a light in the distance and, having alerted the rest, they made their way to a small peasant dwelling. A hesitant knock at the door produced an equally hesitant response. The rickety wooden door opened slowly, and they were confronted by a family of peasants, huddled in the middle of the room, frightened perhaps as much as they were. In the meantime, my mother had suffered a miscarriage, and her ashen face and bedraggled appearance led the woman of the house to urge her in and offered her a chair. Without much discussion among themselves, they had authorized Roufa to explain who they were. They were members of a band of black marketeers from Thrace and Macedonia, he said, on the run from the authorities; their friends were hiding a few hundred paces away. Was it my mother's pitiful appearance, or was it perhaps their new identity as underground traders, or perhaps some other reason? The fact is that they were let in, offered a spare room to rest in, with my mother invited to lie down on a sort of straw mattress.

Four or five hours had passed since they had left home. Today, it would not take even one hour to drive the distance from Salonica to where, approximately, they had been stranded. For them that distance was measured in light years. They had entered an alien world, of concealment and dissimulation, of false identities and of inhabiting not simply the margins, but the darkest corners of the margins, where people who are hunted slink along in the hope they will not be spotted and recognized for who they really are. Their identity as black marketeers was a sort of badge of honor among those who live in the world of the underground. But no inquiry had been made so far about their names. Who were they? The question would be answered in a semi-official way only several days later when they reached Làrissa. For the moment, they were at the mercy of a family of peasants, who might have been trustworthy or might not. In the middle of the night, for all their fear and exhaustion, unable to sleep, they overheard the whispers of their new hosts. One of them had guessed who they were: Jews who, if turned in to the authorities, would have been worth some money to them. Others were more cautious, hesitant to invite German soldiers or Greek gendarmes into their isolated dwelling. In the end, an agreement was reached: the runaways would not be allowed to stay with them but would be turned over to one of the bands of resistance fighters operating in the mountains. And so it was. The next morning, one of the peasants made contact with the underground, and they all trooped slowly up the mountain, everyone on foot, except for my mother who had been put in a cart pushed by a couple of the mountain people who had hosted them during the first night of their escape.

The next several days—perhaps as much as two or three weeks—were full of the same dangers and uncertainties. The group was handed over from one resistance team to another, as each band controlled a small area, a mountain side or a small, isolated valley, hidden from inquisitive eyes of occupiers or collaborators. As I listened to my mother recounting to me this fairy-tale-like story, I wondered as I was getting older about their determination to stick it out, to suffer appalling hardships, unimagined to people used to the comforts of a middle-class existence with helpers tending to the details of daily life. Whenever I asked my mother about this, she answered that not for a moment did they consider returning to Salonica. They were determined to escape. They knew, she insisted, that a return was equivalent to death.

Why did they know this? What armed them with such grit and confidence? They had left Salonica just days after the first convoy of Jews had departed for Poland. That, surely, was a worrying sign. But it was hardly an omen of what was about to happen. Who could have guessed what was in store for Salonica's Jews? Mass murders of Jews, of the sort one now knows had taken place in Poland and in the Ukraine, had yet to reach the notice of Jews in Salonica. Yet, a deep-seated suspicion, a sort of prescient feeling drove them away from home and kept driving them toward a destination they hoped would be more secure. I think I know what might explain their behavior. It is something that had happened in the summer of 1942, a traumatic event that marked my father, and indirectly my mother, for the following years.

In July 1942, the German authorities convened all adult Jewish males to gather in Plateia Eleftherias (Freedom Square), one of the city's principal open spaces, very close to the port. It is where, a few years ago, the municipal authorities placed a monument in memory of the Jews' deportation by the Germans; it is in that very spot that sympathizers of the extreme right now regularly converge to deface the monument! A police guard now protects the site in memory of the city's Jews murdered in Auschwitz. Every time I pass this spot, an idle thought almost instinctively crosses my mind: How much more useful to the Jews themselves and to the reputation of Greek society it would have been if such police protection had been offered in 1942, when no institutional force had been present to shield them from the violence of the Germans. My father, unlike a few other Jews among whom his two brothers who, shrewdly, either played dumb or simply hid in their homes or at their places of work, on 11 July (the eve of my third birthday, when, obviously, I was not aware of anything that was happening,) showed up at the square early in the morning. There, he soon became aware of the Germans' plan: to keep the few thousand men in the open, under the hot summer sun, and essentially torture them by having them perform demanding physical exercises. Contemporary photos, taken by German soldiers, show the men obeying the Germans' commands. By chance, my father appears in one of these photos, alongside two other men, all of them knees bent, and arms extended straight in front of their chests. Those who hesitated or did not quite meet the standard of their exacting torturers were either subjected to even more rigorous exercises or simply beaten up. My father, under the illusion that his familiarity with German culture and his command of German might give him an advantage in that unpleasant situation, decided to engage one of the soldiers in conversation, trying to find out what it was all about. The result was that he was called out in front of the gathered crowd and severely beaten, a couple of ribs broken and other evident signs of his maltreatment left on his body. Some bystanders picked him up, loaded him in one of those push carts used by port workers to carry sacks of wheat or bales of cloth, and carried him first to a hospital and then home, where it took him several weeks to recover.

The lesson had been learned: He would not trust Germans, notwithstanding his past admiration and respect for their literature and culture. It was impossible to reason with them, however good his German was, and regardless of the German friends he had before the war. One of the consequences of that bitter experience, and of everything that was to follow, was that, after the war, most of his German books were packed and stored away so that nobody could see them, he hardly ever spoke in German (at least I never heard him do it) and, perhaps most crucially for me, he went out of his way not to encourage me to learn German, always finding an excuse for giving precedence to my piano lessons or my lessons in French and English. I well remember a day in the mid-1950s, a few days after I had received my report card from school, when Mr. Frangistas, then Chancellor of the University of Thessaloniki and distinguished jurist, came to lunch at home. He wanted to know how I was doing at school, and my father proudly asked me to show him my report card. Our guest was duly impressed and immediately offered his advice about my studies. After the gymnasium he said, Tony should continue his studies in a German university, preferably Heidelberg, where distinguished Greek jurists and politicians, among them Konstantine Tsatsos and Panayotis Kanellopoulos had studied in the 1920s and 1930s. German universities, he continued, were so much better than those in other parts of the world. His comment was a sign of his desire to offer a bit of helpful advice, but it also bespoke a touch of insensitivity, a lack of understanding of how Jews, especially Salonican Jews, might feel about Germany and German society. My parents interrupted. My father thought that I should continue my studies in Greece. But my mother, peremptorily, as was her custom when the subject of my studies ever came up, added that, if at all possible, I should continue my studies in the United States. That is, she added, if he is good enough to be accepted by a good university. In any case, this painful experience, on that hot summer day in July 1942, was decisive in my father's steely determination to leave, as soon as news of the Germans' intention to transport Salonica's Jews north began to circulate. Better to make a run for it, whatever the risks, than to trust German promises of a new homeland in unknown regions of northern Europe. I think this was a fundamental reason for my parents' persistence not even to consider going back home or quitting.

The escapees were bounced around for several days, from one resistance band to another. On some nights, they felt a little less uncomfortable, on others the uncertainties and dangers overwhelmed them. My mother thought that nearly always this band of six were recognized for what they were: Jews fleeing from the Germans, not simply black marketeers escaping Greek authorities; but in the countryside and in the mountains, their Jewishness did not weigh either for or against them. It was sufficient that they were running away from the law. For this reason alone, they deserved some help. Interestingly, she also thought that, especially among women they met on the way, her presence as a woman predisposed their hosts more favorably to them. It was unclear to me why this was so; was it a sort of female solidarity or perhaps the traditional code of honor in Greece, where women, especially married ones, are treated with deference and respect? Crossing the mountain was tough, but neither impossible nor debilitating. Nothing stopped them from making slow progress toward Làrissa, where they hoped to catch a train and move, more rapidly and comfortably, toward Athens. Although my mother's memory was shaky about precise dates and the passage of time, she thought it took them about three weeks to reach their destination. Is it possible she exaggerated the length of the trip? Difficult to know.

The next stage of their adventure also proved more complicated than they had imagined. In Làrissa, my father, hoping to find help, located an old customer, to whom he appealed for assistance. His hopes were only half met. Help was, indeed, offered but reluctantly and with great hesitation. Unlike country folk, people in urban areas, even acquaintances, were afraid of being compromised and getting themselves and their families in trouble, especially by jealous and suspicious neighbors. But my father's acquaintance put them up in his house for a few days, thus giving the weary travelers a short respite, a chance to take a bath and change clothes. The other members of the traveling group—my two uncles and the two other family friends—found accommodations elsewhere, but they all agreed to stick together and continue as a group in their southward trek. The object was to get to Athens, hopefully by train, which they could board in Làrissa. My parents' reluctant host charged his two sons to look into ways of helping his guests, and the two young men came up with what was needed to satisfy everyone: relieve their parents of the burden of providing hospitality for their unwelcome visitors and make it possible for the group of six to travel by train to their destination.

In those days, you could travel by train only if you had a valid, police-issued, identity card, which included not only the usual information about the holder's and parents' names, birth date, and physical information, but also the person's religious affiliation written under her or his name. Interestingly, this requirement was lifted only about a couple of dozen years ago, so that, every time I used my Greek ID, seeing the term "Israelite" written below my name, I remembered my parents' difficult moments in Làrissa, as they were stuck in a not altogether hospitable home for the arrival of their false papers. But even if their religious identity had been omitted from their old papers, their very names would have given them away: Saul Molho, son of Lazar and Lily Alkalay Molho, daughter of Nissim, both born in Salonica, were markers enough of their Jewishness. Obviously, their regular identity cards would not do, fresh ones had to be found, with new, invented names inscribed on them. The names were, indeed, found: Savas Panayotidis for my father, Eleni Panayotidou for my mother. Why did they settle on these names? In her recounting, my mother explained that Panayotidis was chosen more or less at random, pulled out of a hat, as my father once said; as for Savas, although more of a Slavic name, it could also pass as Greek, and, in any case, it was close to Saul so my father could remember it with little difficulty. Eleni, one of the commonest women's names in Greece, was sufficiently similar to Lily that she accepted it without protest.

As it was, the young men were sent on an errand to explore ways of obtaining—for a price—new IDs. They came back with the much-valued prizes, including valid train tickets. Crucially, under their new names, the two key words were clearly written: "Christian Orthodox." In those days, not only in Làrissa, there was a thriving black market for false identity papers, and that is where my parents' new IDs were purchased. Their public transformation was now complete, authorized, it would seem, by the Greek state itself in whose name these documents were issued. They had become new people. Thanks to their new identity papers, their old personae were pushed somewhere in the back of their consciousness, and they felt more or less free to dissimulate their new identity. For years after the war, these false identity cards were tucked away at home together with other papers: old ID cards, school records, old photos. Then, at some point, probably after one of our moves, they disappeared. I wish I still had them in my possession. They were the only tangible proof of my parents' escape from home and of their long trek, across much of Greece, during the war. I would be curious today to see their faces in the pictures stamped on their ID cards. Did these photographs convey their features as I remember them from later years—my mother's sharp eyes and the determination that was a permanent feature of her face, and my father's more pensive look, his seemingly more placid personality? But these documents do not exist. The next best evidence of my parents' appearances during those years are the identity cards issued very shortly after their return home, my father's on 2 July 1945 and my mother's on 19 January 1946. Her religion was listed as "Israelite." My father's, thanks to a bureaucrat's accommodating attitude toward German terminology, was listed as "Mosaic." In Làrissa, with their new ID cards in hand, they were free to move about at will. Suffice it that some mishap not give them away or that some technical imperfection in the new documents not raise someone's suspicion. Predictably, such a snafu would soon arise.

The last leg of the trip to Athens proved to be at once the easiest and the most adventuresome and dangerous. As I am writing these lines, I am struck by the naturalness with which my parents used a strategy of concealment meant to maximize their chances of survival. Was this strategy nurtured by their familiarity with spy and mystery movies and novels, which my mother certainly often enjoyed after the war and probably also before? Perhaps. The fact is that, once in the station, waiting for the train to arrive, they decided to sit as far apart from each other as possible, my mother in one carriage, my father in another, with my two uncles sitting in my mother's carriage, but distant from her. Their intent, as my mother later recounted,

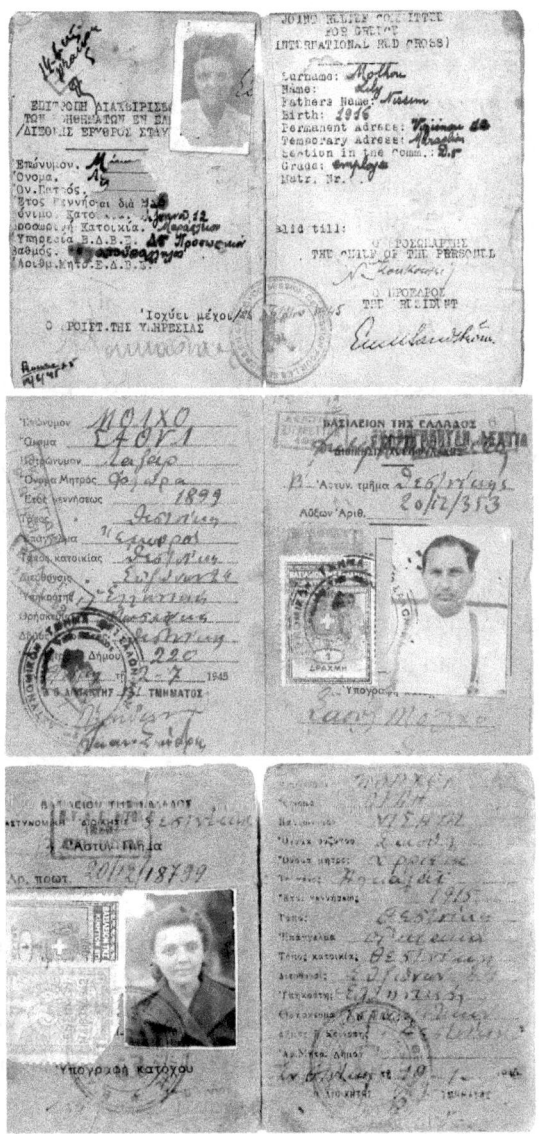

Figure 4.1. *(a) Three immediate postwar documents. My mother's Red Cross ID, 1945. (b) My father's police ID card, 2 July 1945, with his religion listed as "Mosaic." (c) My mother's police ID, 19 January 1946.*

was to ensure that, for my sake, in case one of them was caught, the other had a better chance to arrive safely in Athens. The train was jammed, so they remained unobserved, and were able to pass with no difficulty the first controller's routine examination of their tickets and documents. A little before reaching Lamia, a second controller came through.

Without question, the next hour or so was the most dramatic, high-stakes gamble in my mother's attempt to survive. Walking toward their destination, stumbling along at a speed of no more than 5 kilometers an hour, over often impossibly tough roads, proved to be a lot safer than hurtling along in a train, at 40–50 kilometers an hour. In the countryside, you had the chance to run away, to hide, even to stop to catch your breath. In the train, you were stuck. For all the comfort of sitting down and looking at the scenery as the train sped along, you could not easily hide from the inquisitive gaze of an overly curious fellow passenger or of an inspector or policeman.

Unfortunately, this is what happened. The second controller's punctiliousness precipitated a near catastrophe. It did not take long for him to realize that my mother's ID was a forgery. In those times, traveling with false papers was no misdemeanor; it was a major, punishable crime. For a Jew, the crime was punishable not by the Greek authorities but by the German occupiers. My mother's papers were confiscated. She was placed under arrest and told that in a little while the train would arrive in Lamia, and she would be turned over to the German command. What happened next was worthy of the best suspense novel my mother read in the comfort of her home in Evzonon Street. Her instinct for survival, her fear that all her and her companions' sacrifices and hardships in the previous weeks would have been for naught, and her panic that her son would be left motherless in the care of unknown people, touched her fierce determination. Instead of panicking or crying, she fought back. There was little more she could now lose. Please let me talk to the chief engineer, she asked. Surprisingly, the controller consented. So, the two, followed by the horrified looks of her two brothers-in-law who had the good sense not to say or do anything, crossed the length of the train and finally found the engineer. He repeated to her what she had been told by the controller. The law required him to turn her over to the German command in Lamia, and he intended to follow the law.

My mother looked at him squarely in the eyes and asked him if he had family and children. Yes, he did, he answered, he was the father of two children. I also have a son, said my mother. Summoning all her emotion and her courage, she hissed at him with the calm and determined intensity that only desperation could engender. If you turn me in to the Germans, my son will be orphaned of his mother. And if that happens, may my curse forever be on your children. It was as if a scene of an ancient Greek play was being performed. Only this was not an ancient Greek play, it was a contemporary Greek drama. It seems hard to believe that such a searing, surreally intense exchange could have taken place under those circumstances. Two parents faced each other, each overwhelmed by the thought that something horrible might happen to their children, both stretched their minds and wills to understand how they should respond to each other. The man was thunderstruck upon hearing the threat of such a curse—so thought my mother later. He hesitated for a few moments and, because at heart he was a good man, added my mother as she recounted to me this story, he relented. I'll try to help you, he told her. And so, in this confrontation of two parents, the children's well-being, and their very future lives won out.

How could a however well-intentioned engineer help a Jewish woman, traveling with false papers, whom the German command would have loved to put their hands on? There seemed to be only one way out: make her disappear from sight, put her in a place where no German patrol could think of looking for her. So, engineer that he was, he began reducing the speed of the train, and at a certain moment as the train continued to move, he opened the door, waved to my mother to step outside on the external running board, and urged her to hold on for life. He closed the door and asked three of his friends to stand in front of the door so as to block anyone from observing the outside scenery. Then, the train once again picked up speed. My mother was hanging on for dear life, the train whistle kept blowing, the three men in front of the door lit cigarettes and slightly rolled down the window to let their smoke escape to the outside, but, in truth, claimed my mother later, to continue observing her in the hope that she was safe. And as the train was speeding faster, on the pretense of making up time it had lost, my mother hung on, too dazed to think about what was happening. The German patrol stationed in the train came by, checked everyone's papers, and moved on. The danger had passed. Once again, the train started slowing down, the door leading to the platform was opened again, and my mother was helped by her saviors as she stepped back into the carriage.

The rest of the trip to Athens, perhaps as much as four hours long, was uneventful. Later on, after the war, Uncle Isaac (who at that time was Uncle Yannis) quipped that they had already had enough excitement—they needed no more adventures. So, on a sunny afternoon in mid-April 1943, not quite one month after bidding farewell to Salonica, the band of six escapees, four of whom were Molhos, arrived in Athens. They were exhausted, filthy, frightened but also relieved beyond words, and unsure what was in store for them. But then, unexpectedly, something pleasant happened. Among the crowd milling about in the train station, my father spotted Mr. Naar, by far his closest friend in Salonica. Together with wife and son (about five years older than me), the Naars had made their way to Athens a little earlier and settled in a home somewhere near the city center. Every day, it seems, Mr. Naar would wander to the train station, in anticipation of spotting someone he knew who might be arriving from Salonica. No sooner did the two old friends meet, than an invitation to my parents was extended to stay with the Naars until they, also, could find proper accommodations.

It has taken me almost as long to record the memory of this adventure as it took my parents and their companions to travel from Salonica to Athens. I so much wish my mother could have read this chapter. My father died so many years ago, decades before I had begun to ponder the idea of writing this memoir. It was with my mother I often talked about this story, and I think it is fair to say that she would have been my ideal reader. Her mind remained sharp until only a few weeks before her death well past her ninety-first birthday, and I am sure that she would not have hesitated a moment to tell me her impressions of what I wrote. For my part, I would have tried to draw her out on my reflections about this story. Would she have agreed with me? I am not sure. Quite beyond the spectacularly impressive quality of her story, there is another idea to which I returned time and again as I was writing these pages. Surely, my parents had made it to Athens because of their remarkable courage and determination, also because at some crucial moments *Fortuna*, the Roman goddess of good luck, *Tyche* as we say in Greek, had smiled on them. Without the helping hand that, time and again, they were offered by some simple folk, chances are that they would not have made it. My mother would not have denied this. But her grief at her own family's fate led her to the bitter thought that no one in Salonica had helped them, that not only the Germans but also collectively the city's entire Christian (what she would call, the Greek) population were responsible for the extermination of Salonica's Jewish population. It is possible that she was not entirely wrong. Sharp tensions, even enmities, had built up in Salonica between the city's by now ancient Sephardic community that, in 1941 counted perhaps more than 55,000 Jews and the Greek Orthodox Christians, perhaps twice as many as the Jews, a good number of whom, following the massive Greek defeat in the war against Turkey in 1922, had arrived penniless and eager to put down roots in that city. Jews and their properties were seen as easy prey, to be elbowed into the arms of the German occupiers, their goods appropriated without much ado. Remember the story of the yellow curtain?

I would have retorted that her salvation and that of my father can also be credited in large part to the good actions of many simple Greeks, in scattered settlements across Mount Olympus, middle-class folk in Làrissa, passengers and engineers in a crowded train on its way to Athens. They were also Greeks, but perhaps significantly not Greeks from Salonica, who, for whatever reason, chose to expose themselves to considerable risk and offer a helping hand. In thinking about the question I asked myself in an earlier chapter—what does it mean for me to be a Greek Jew—my parents' extraordinary trip from Salonica to Athens in the spring of 1943 offers a powerful corrective to my mother's view that tended to see us not so much as Greek Jews but as Jews who happened to be living in Greece.

5.

Soeur Hélène

"Would you rather go back and stay with Soeur Hélène?" I can still hear my mother's half serious, half joking voice, while I was cringing in some corner, having done or said something she did not approve of in the first few years after the war. We were by then in Salonica, sorting out our lives: my mother trying to come to terms with her immense personal losses and facing, as best she could, the nervous collapse that plagued her for years; my father looking for the energy to restart his business all the while fumbling about on how to manage my mother's illness; while I, following two years of floating about in Salonica and Athens, was called upon to adjust to the pleasures and constraints of family life. There were few constants in our confused and confusing lives. Of these, by far the most important were the raw memories of recent events. Soeur Hélène was a protagonist in these memories.

Until my parents' arrival in Athens in April 1943, no one in the family had ever heard of Hélène Capart, who, in Greece, was more generally known as Soeur Hélène or Adelphì Eleni (Sister Eleni). For all our ignorance of her existence, were it not for Soeur Hélène, our lives would in all likelihood have taken a very different, perhaps a much less happy turn. Soeur Hélène was a Catholic nun, Belgian in origin, daughter of a distinguished classical archaeologist. By the time my parents met her in late spring of 1943, she had taken religious vows, and become the Mother Superior of the Catholic convent Pammakaristos in Patissia, near the center of Athens. There, she presided over a community of perhaps as many as two dozen Greek-speaking Catholic nuns, who hailed mostly from the islands of Syros and Tinos, remnants of a long bygone era of Venetian and Genoese domination. Her order also ran a sort of hostel in the very heart of Athens for single women who had moved to the city from the provinces in search of work. It also operated an elementary school located next door to the convent, which, during the war, was converted into a neighborhood hospital and more recently transformed into a large and modern hospital. In the last forty or so years, religious vocations having greatly declined, the number of nuns at the old convent fell, and sometime in the 1980s, the remaining half dozen nuns, many of them old and infirm, moved to a very pleasant estate—donated by a well-to-do patron—in the posh northern suburb of Kifissià, where I used to visit them while Soeur Hélène was alive. In my last visit there, a dozen or so years ago, four nuns were left, the oldest of whom was younger than me! The memory of the convent's problems during the war was largely faded, the surviving nuns asking me for information about my recollections of Soeur Hélène and the other nuns whom I had met in 1943.

In the early 1940s, Soeur Hélène had become a well-known figure in Athens. She was connected with political authorities, among them the Chief of Athens Police Angelos Evert and, largely thanks to her father's archaeological activities in Greece during the 1930s, with some important scholars and intellectuals. She also worked closely on social and relief matters with the primate of Greece Archbishop Damaskinos, a remarkable religious figure, whose open support of Greek Jews in 1943 so angered the German authorities, that they threatened to have him shot by a firing squad. This physically imposing and politically engaged figure had established continuous if surreptitious contacts with the Greek underground whose units, by the beginning of 1943, were carrying out often successful raids on the German and Italian occupation forces. The friendship between Soeur Hélène and Archbishop Damaskinos was remarkable in light of the traditionally intense antagonism, often exploding in outbursts of embarrassing rivalry between Greek Orthodox Christians and Catholic Christians; resentments rooted in events of 1204 and the Fourth Crusade when the Venetians looted many important monuments in Constantinople had been systematically cultivated by Greek Orthodox priests and theologians. These two remarkable figures had been able to overlook these rivalries and worked closely together to combat the common enemy: the Axis.

The links between Soeur Hélène, Archbishop Damaskinos, and the underground proved vital for our family's survival. In the case of my father, the Archbishop's contacts with the Greek underground of ELAS (Greek People's Liberation Army) offered him the chance to escape from Athens and join the partisans in the mountains of central Greece. But Soeur Hélène also provided the necessary cover to help me get through the following very difficult months and, thanks to her social connections, contributed mightily to my mother's successful concealment until the early months of 1944.

My parents decided it was best that I be moved to Athens, and live somewhere near them. Arrangements for my trip to

Athens had been made, and now it was time to find a safe hideout. It turned out to be a much more difficult challenge than my parents had anticipated. No one in the family had any useful contacts in Athens, certainly they knew no one who could have been entrusted with as delicate and dangerous a task as concealing a little Jewish boy. Although roundups of Jews in Athens had not begun systematically, there were signs that Germans intended to apply the same policy to Jews living in Athens as they had done in Salonica. Sometime between my parents' arrival and mine in Athens, Mr. Naar, my father's very good friend (the one who had chanced on my parents in the train station), had been arrested. His wife and son managed to jump out of a back window just as German soldiers were bursting in their house, but he had not escaped; predictably, he was sent to Auschwitz where he was murdered. In the last few days before her escape from Salonica, someone had mentioned to my mother that if ever she needed help in Athens, she should seek out Madame Kallinus, wife of a Belgian consular official, who, rumor had it, was kindly inclined toward Jews and willing to help them. So, once arrangements for my trip to Athens were made, the search started for a safe home where I could be hidden. My mother had sought out Mme. Kallinus who had suggested that a convent would be a proper place for me to hide. A religious community would not easily be suspected, especially one where refugees and orphans were ordinarily sheltered. So, starting early one morning, the two of them, Mme. Kallinus and my mother, began canvassing the numerous convents throughout Athens. Each visit lasted only a few minutes, and the answer throughout was negative. Each Mother Superior regretted her inability to help—so she said. If only Tony had been a girl, they would have taken me in with no hesitation. But a physical examination by

COURAGE AND COMPASSION

any police official or German soldier would have shown that I was Jewish. The risk was too great for the nuns. The mood changed when they arrived at the Pammakaristos. I am unsure if, in recounting her version of the story, my mother embellished her recollection or if, indeed, things went as smoothly as she claimed.

No sooner had they been introduced to her and explained their mission, Soeur Hélène understood the problem. It was essential to provide cover for the little boy. She accepted the risk as part of her religious duty. Speaking in French, she tried to calm my mother who, understandably, was agitated and sought reassurances that no one could have given her. Soeur Hélène spoke quietly and authoritatively and, as she often did in later years when I visited her, laced her speech with simple religious ideas that underscored the need for human beings to help each other. *Nous sommes tous enfants du Créateur* is a phrase I remember her saying to me after the war in my occasional visits to her, and I would not be surprised if she said something very similar in her conversation with my mother. Repeatedly in recalling this meeting, my mother would confess in wonderment that, in the course of that encounter, she had witnessed a miracle. She obviously meant that the outcome of her discussion with Soeur Hélène was unexpected—especially after her earlier experience that day. But, even without perhaps clearly acknowledging this to herself, I think she may also have meant that Soeur Hélène's appearance, her demeanor, even her very words conveyed something transcendent, something almost holy. She was fairly young—perhaps then in her early 40s—tall and slender, wearing her order's simple working habit, her face framed by a wimple that highlighted her soft if serious smile, she gave the appearance of someone belonging to a different universe. I thought I was in the presence of an angel, thought my mother. The middle-class Sephardic world of Salonica, in which my mother had been nurtured, with its concrete values rooted in commerce and cultural achievements, left little room for altruism and abnegation, much less for self-sacrifice, except, no doubt, for members of one's own family. Soeur Hélène personified these values. Hers was a Christian world far removed from the harsh, exclusionary ideology of the Greek Orthodox Christian universe of Salonica and its surroundings. For years thereafter, in Greece and in the United States, my mother harked back to Soeur Hélène's example. If the war's disasters had shaped her attitude and hardened her character, the memory of Soeur Hélène served to somewhat soften that harshness, to make her always sensitive to other people's plight and to one's responsibility to those in need. In later years, her quiet support of Palestinian children was no doubt in large measure inspired by the memory of Soeur Hélène and by the risk she had willingly assumed to hide me.

In the course of this first encounter, Soeur Hélène had someone brought into her office and introduced to my mother. She was Mrs. Fanni Kalkou, a widow, who with her five young children lived nearby and did odd jobs at the convent. The Mother Superior explained to Mrs. Kalkou the situation and forewarned her that she might be called upon for help if, for any reason at all, the convent's newest guest had to be moved out and sheltered somewhere else. It proved to be an auspicious warning, because several weeks later such an emergency would arise. My mother was obviously grateful to both women for their generosity and courage. But she was especially struck by the nun's urging to the widow. "You have five children," she told Mrs. Kalkou. "A sixth mouth to feed will not make a big difference." For years afterward, my mother remembered the soft smile with which Mrs. Kalkou responded to the Mother Superior's urging. These two women, a nun and a widow, might well have been centerpieces of a fictional account of adventure, uncertainty, and salvation. Only this was reality.

So, with proper shelter secured, a day or two after my arrival in Athens I was led to the convent of Pammakaristos. As in the cases of my two previous transfers to new homes, I do not remember any details of my arrival there. It must have been sometime in June (1943), shortly before my fourth birthday. Nor, I confess, do I remember much of my life there, in the months before my removal to Mrs. Kalkou's house. The convent has remained in my memory a dark place, long, silent, windowless corridors, an alcove close to a door where Soeur Anastasie, the nun who was charged with looking after me, would on occasion sit me on a low stool and, away from inquisitive eyes, feed me a raw egg beaten with a spoonful of sugar. In the autumn of 1943, a period of deadly famine in the city, anything that was different from a piece of bread and some dried beans seemed a gourmet specialty. Hunger drove me, and the egg tasted delicious. Yet, the aftertaste of those raw eggs has stayed with me over the years, and I have been unable to eat a raw egg since. Nor do I have an image of where I slept, whether in a room alone or in a space I shared with others.

I do recall on some days (it must have been on Sundays and holidays) being in the convent chapel where I listened to the Mass. The ritual, the chanting (that I do not recall clearly but which was in Latin during Mass, but most probably in Greek in litanies), the short processions, the music played on a small, portable organ, perhaps also the presence of all the nuns gathered in one place must have intrigued me. Much later, I was told that occasionally I was called upon to carry out small tasks during Mass, but I have no recollection of this. I retain a very vague, misty memory of this ritual that, even if it did not mostly engage me directly, must have attracted me for its strangeness and its formal, predictable routine. As far as I remember, the nuns made no systematic effort to indoctrinate me. In their eyes, attending Mass must have been a sort of socializing to help me adjust to my new environment. I may be wrong about this and have wondered if my life-long fascination with the history of Christianity was not born because these images and sounds of the Mass were first inscribed in my mind. After the war, in our visits to Soeur Hélène, my mother did not refrain from occasionally making passing quips about my participation in these masses.

In the meantime, Soeur Hélène was at work to help my parents. Her connections with Archbishop Damaskinos were quickly put to use to help my father. Of the three of us he was probably the most vulnerable, speaking, as he did to the end of his days, with the lilting pronunciation of Salonica's Sephardic Jews. Damaskinos was alerted by Soeur Hélène about my father's plight, and he in turn communicated with one of the underground units not far from Athens. So, one night, the Archbishop's chauffeured car picked up my father and drove him to his destination. This was the last my mother heard from him from June 1943 to October 1944. It was as if he had been swallowed up by the mountains and by the partisan groups who were fighting the German and Italian armies. And then, as quietly as he had left, in the middle of a night in mid-October 1944, just as the civil war was to engulf Greece, he reappeared at the house where my mother and I were living. A few weeks before his reappearance, my mother, torn by the uncertainty about his fate, had managed to convince a British soldier—one of the first to have arrived near Athens just as the Germans were retreating—to take her on a ride to the mountains surrounding Athens where it was known that units of the resistance were operating. Climbing on the back of a motorcycle—her first and last motorcycle ride in her life—the two of them ventured to a number of hideouts controlled by the resistance. No one had any useful information about my father. In the course of the day, she picked up a rumor that someone who seemed to fit his description had died several months before, another one reported that Savas (my father's false name) had taken very ill but was unsure of his fate, but the majority of the partisans my mother talked with simply did not know. I remember well her return to the house late on the day of her adventure, exhausted, and crying. Another of her silent and anonymous heroes for years thereafter was the English soldier, who had offered his help for no compensation or personal advantage but simply out of a feeling of pity and kindness.

It seems that at every turn in our forbiddingly difficult saga, someone turned up to offer vital help and save the day: a few soldiers, first the two German soldiers billeted in our house, then an English soldier offering a helping hand to my mother; a Catholic nun; a Greek Orthodox bishop; a poor widow; a train conductor and a railway engineer; and, before and after, families that were willing to take me alone or together with my mother to hide us. It was a cross section of humanity that stands in sharp contrast to another cross section of humanity—German officials, soldiers, and Greek collaborators who tortured and killed Jews and others; avid, simple folk who could not wait to enrich themselves by grabbing the property of those who were being persecuted and then feigned not to know where their wealth had come from; bigoted and unethical clerics who could not imagine—indeed, could not tolerate the thought of—a world that was beyond the limits of their prejudices.

No doubt, we were lucky. I do not think it was only luck that helped us, even if, echoing one of my favorite thinkers, I have to admit that *Fortuna* was on our side. But our good luck I think was also the outcome of my parents' own willingness to take risks—to risk by entrusting their only child to unknown people, to risk by escaping and abandoning home and hearth and family and a well-known life, to risk by facing down collaborators, to risk by leading a life of dissimulation. They paid a high price for their survival. But they survived.

My father was a reticent and very quiet person. In conversations with him after the war, we could on occasion squeeze from him details of his prewar experiences—especially about his favorite hobby, which was mountain climbing through northern Greece, and his one great exploit in the early 1930s before he had met my mother, having been a passenger in the first international flight from Salonica's primitive airport to Vienna, where he had traveled to attend the opera. But about his wartime experiences he was silent. It was as if his almost year and a half of scrambling about in the countryside, laden with a gun that, I suspect, he did not have much of an idea how to use, socializing with men and women whose lives had been very different from his own, being a witness, perhaps even a participant, in occasional combat encounters with Italian and German soldiers—as if all that experience had vanished from his mind. More probably, he did not want to share it with us. The war and his own direct involvement in it had nothing of the heroic about it. Still, my mother would on occasion teasingly refer to two incidents that penetrated his silences.

COURAGE AND COMPASSION

One took place in October 1944, when he reappeared after his long absence. He quietly made his way to our house in the middle of the night and first sought directions from the next-door neighbor who, very discretely, walked over to our house and softly tapped on the window of our room to alert us that an unexpected visitor had just shown up. When he, himself, sauntered over, he was some kind of a spectacle. His sheepish smile could not cover his appearance: he was filthy, his body and his clothes covered with lice, his shoes torn, his hair and beard long and untended. Your father was the perfect image of a derelict, my mother used to say. Once the shock of recognition had passed, he was led to the bathroom where, with my mother's help and with the assistance of the two other ladies of the house, he was scrubbed down with hot water that was being heated in the kitchen and brought to the bathroom in tin buckets. I remember all that. My mother and I were by then sharing a room, and I heard it all, although I hardly understood the reason for the commotion that had awakened me. I recall wondering to myself what this unknown man was doing in our room conversing with my mother in a strange language—Ladino or French—that I did not understand.

Another memory—as so much else in this small book—is tied to a photograph. It is a photo that was in the family's possession until we first arrived in Cleveland, in August 1956. Since then, I have looked for it many times to no avail. My sister used to tell me that, surely, it must still be somewhere among the myriad things my mother got in the habit of amassing, in drawers, cupboards, closets, in the attic and the basement, even among books, where we could find newspaper clippings, photographs that came her way, old letters, even her driver's licenses that she much prized, since she had learned to drive only after our arrival in the United States. The fact is that I have been unable to find this picture, and its loss greatly saddens me. On more than one occasion when I was a boy, I would sit and stare at it, trying to imagine who the people in the picture were and what role my father had in the group. The picture was most probably taken in spring or summer of 1944, but I have no idea who took it, with whose camera, and where it was developed and printed. These questions continue to puzzle me. It showed about two dozen partisans, both men and women, in a moment of relaxation. Standing or crouching around a row of somewhat bedraggled looking people lying in the front row, they all seem at ease, some of them smiling, a few bearing arms, others having rested their guns on the ground, some wearing a semblance of uniforms, others simple civilian clothes. My father was stretched out on the ground, with a trace of a smile on his face, a gun, perhaps his own, resting a small distance in front of him. It was a nice image of the often-ramshackle nature of the Greek resistance, which, for all its undeniable occasional successes, was not terribly (or not always) well organized.

This picture was the one tangible evidence of my father's participation in the resistance. It also offered my mother more than one occasion to tease him about those sixteen or so months of his absence. Who were those women, she used to ask him. How well did you get to know them? Which one was your favorite? The teasing did not go beyond this point, if for no other reason but for my father's shyness. When I was about ten, on a Sunday stroll in the country, for reasons I do not remember, my mother impishly started her teasing. Uncle Isaac, who by now had shed his name of Yannis, joined the conversation: *Addiò Lily, déjalo en paz,* (For God's sake, Lily, leave him in peace) don't you see that this subject embarrasses him? I was still too young to un-

Figure 5.1. *Two pictures, both taken in 1956, shortly before our departure for the United States: (a) My father, (b) My mother.*

derstand why the subject embarrassed my father. But it did, and this picture and its postwar life shed a tiny bit of light into the black hole of his absence during the German occupation of Greece.

Many years later, when we were established in Cleveland, in the immediate aftermath of the MacCarthy era and of Father Couglin's violently antisemitic radio broadcasts, my father's participation in the resistance proved to be an unexpected obstacle to his integration in his new country. It seems that when in November 1961 my parents applied on behalf of all four of us for US citizenship, my father's application was held up because of suspicions expressed by someone in the Immigration Office about his reliability as a good US citizen. Might he have been sympathetic to the Communist Party? Had he maintained ties with his comrades in the mountains, who, in the meantime, had tried but failed to stage a revolution in Greece? This episode, nearly two decades after the end of the war, deeply hurt my father. He had reluctantly consented to my mother's insistence to leave Greece to settle in the United States and simply assumed that his record as a law-abiding citizen in Greece was sufficient guarantee of his suitability to adjust to his new life. Not unreasonably, he imagined that his participation in the resistance would be seen at once as an act of self-defense and of patriotism. He had never imagined the distorted logic of American super-patriots who seemed to lack even an elementary idea of the dilemmas a Greek Jew faced during World War II. My mother, who had kept a steady correspondence with Soeur Hélène, wrote to her about this unexpected twist of events and received a puzzled response about the reasons behind the FBI's objections to my father's possible US citizenship. When, a year or two later, my father was finally notified that his application had been approved, Soeur Hélène, who, in the summer of 1943, had, in some way, set in motion this string of events, wrote her congratulations. But by then, my father had become a dispirited and unhappy person, and he died four years later in Cleveland at the relatively young age of sixty-eight.

My father had twice made immense sacrifices in order to help me. First, when he consented to give me up to a new family. Again, a dozen years after the war, when he was fifty-seven years old, he gave in to my mother's pressure to migrate to the United States, thinking that I would have a better future there than in Greece. His first bet had paid off. Whatever doubts he may have had about the second, he kept them to himself, insisting that the second sacrifice was worth it.

The next phase of my mother's experience in Athens was perhaps as improbable as any of the previous ones. In retrospect, it might seem strange that a prominent beer manufacturer's family was implicated in Soeur Hélène's plans for helping my mother. But this is exactly what happened. What follows will perhaps explain why, for years after the war, my family always preferred one particular brand of beer over others.

Until a few years ago, a waiter in any Greek restaurant or tavern was more than likely to ask you a question soon after you sat at your table. Do you want a Fix? What he meant was if you wanted a beer. This question was asked of restaurant patrons for generations, arguably from the middle of the nineteenth century to the 1970s, when Fix lost its beer monopoly. For about a hundred years, Fix had become synonymous with beer. Yet, the name Fix does not simply refer to beer. The beer itself takes its name from the Fix (originally Fuchs) family, one of a band of Bavarian families that followed in the footsteps of Greece's first modern monarch, King Otto of Bavaria, and settled in Athens. There, the Fixes prospered by introducing beer brewing—what else could a Bavarian manufacturer bring to the new kingdom? One can see, even today, fragments of their ambitiously posh summer estate in the northern Athenian suburb of Neo Heraklion. Being Bavarian meant that they were Catholic, and being Catholic, in turn, meant that they were familiar, perhaps even on good terms with Soeur Hélène.

Faced with the urgent need to help my mother, Soeur Hélène's mind turned to the Fixes—they were well-to-do and well connected, friendly to the German occupiers and therefore beyond suspicion, and, perhaps because of a shared religious confession, sensitive to the request of the Mother Superior. Was Mrs. Fix informed that my mother was Jewish? Given the circumstances, it is more than likely that she was. But the point was never made clear, and for many years afterward, my mother was uncertain. Following a few additional telephone calls, my mother was told that she would soon start working at the Fix home as their second cook. A day or two later, one of the Fix cars was sent to the convent, where my mother was picked up and driven to her new employer's summer estate. A standard family joke after the war was that my parents were driven in chauffeured limousines to their hideouts: my father in the Archbishop's car to the mountains, and my mother in the Fix automobile to her new employer's home. Can you imagine, would quip my father, we had two chauffeurs, but we can't even afford to have a car of our own!

Were circumstances not so dangerous, and the situation so full of potentially fatal traps, what followed would have been ironic, if not outright funny. Just think of it: Lily Molho, the cook—no matter if only the second cook! The fact is that at home, before she was married, my mother had made a point of staying far from the kitchen. Her job, she kept saying after the war, had been studying. Having graduated both from Salonica's French school (the Mission Laïque Française) and from the American school (Anatolia College) her passion was the piano, which she practiced as much as eight hours a day, in preparation for her music degree at the National Conservatory in Salonica. Her Diploma from the Conservatory, that hangs on a wall in my house in Athens, reminds me of her priorities and of her excellence in her music avocation. She insisted that she simply had no time, and certainly no interest in cooking. At home, cooking was the responsibility of the family cook, who was assisted from a distance by my grandmother. But being a cook was not quite as daunting a challenge as those she had recently overcome. So, she adapted to the demands of her new job quickly, picking up cooking lessons on the fly, by observing the other kitchen staff. The learning process started immediately, no more than a few hours following her arrival at the Fixes. A big fish was being served for dinner that night, and my mother was led to the kitchen and asked to clean it and prepare to serve it. She was lost! Her uncertainty and her ignorance were so evident that one of the family chauffeurs who happened to be in the kitchen told her not to worry, he would clean the fish and prepare it for the table. She would simply carry the platter with the fish to the dining room and let the guests help themselves. What a relief, would sigh my mother when recalling this small incident! He was such a kind man, and he helped me pass my first test in the kitchen.

Her stay at the Fixes lasted several months and proved more uneventful than one might have expected. Mrs. Fix and other members of the family were distant but polite. No one pressed my mother about why she had sought such a position, nor was there any attempt to delve into her background. After the war, my mother thought that in all likelihood there was a tacit understanding of the need to remain calm and discreet lest her secret be let out. She was probably right. For the moment, a safe hideout seemed to have been found, and that was good enough. Keep your head down, try not to provoke, step away from any situation that might give rise to suspicions. Above all, no talk of family, no reference to her husband from whom no news had arrived, nor about her son who was tucked away in the convent about a dozen kilometers away. After the war, she remembered what a relief it was to once again wear her wedding band, when she finally left the Fix employment! The band itself brought back such nice memories—of her short, married life, after all she had been married less than six years; of family life in Evzonon Street; of the comforts that were so strikingly absent since that fateful day when she and the rest of the gang had slipped out of their cozy world and left for the mountains.

Inevitably, moments of tension would arise. The chief cook, distrustful of her new assistant, kept putting her to the test, assigning to her responsibilities that she suspected could not be discharged by someone as inexperienced as evidently the second cook was. So, a freshly killed chicken was turned over to my mother to unfeather and clean, a feat she proudly recounted many times after the war; or, trays laden with glasses and bottles were given to her to carry to the living room and drinks served to guests, among whom often were German officers. Mrs. Fix knew, perhaps she only sensed, that the assistant cook had other talents that could be put to better use. Most importantly, it was discovered (but I don't know how) that she could offer piano instruction to the Fix children. This new assignment brought an evident improvement in her status although, soon, it created new suspicions about her. How could an inexperienced cook be such a good pianist? Whenever the children were ready for their lessons and no guests were present, my mother would be summoned to the music room, hold her lesson, and, at the end, hurry back to the kitchen. A run-in with the senior cook nearly brought things to a head, when, for whatever reason, my mother absentmindedly wore the stockings in which she had sewn the four gold sovereigns she had brought with her from Salonika. The senior cook spotted the coins and challenged her subordinate to explain; my mother had obvious difficulties to respond, and, from then on whatever food was being prepared, an icy atmosphere prevailed in the kitchen.

After a few weeks at the Fixes, the lady of the house informed my mother that the family were pleased with her, and that they would give her two afternoons a week off. She could do with her free time as she wished, provided her break began after lunch, and ended before dinner was served. This left a little less than six hours of freedom. She could stay in her room or relax in the large garden, or, even, walk to the square of Neo Heraklion, where she could dawdle around the few stores and coffee shops. None of these options attracted her. What she wanted to do was to find a way to check up on her son. The Fix estate was about twelve kilometers from the convent, not exactly around the corner. Because of frequent police controls in public buses, traveling by bus was not advisable. The only option was to walk, although on a few occasions the family chauffeur would spot her on the road and offer to take her part of the way. Her explanation to those who asked, was that she wanted to visit an elderly aunt who was unwell.

Twice a week, my mother walked for more than two hours each way, to spend about twenty to thirty minutes watching me from afar. Soeur Hélène and the other nuns thought it would be best for mother and son not come in direct contact—this would not happen until later. I do not recall these visits. My mother would sit quietly in a corner where she could observe me, unnoticed by me. After at most half an hour—enough time to satisfy herself that I was well and to catch her breath—rain or shine, she set on her way back. This difficult round-trip was repeated two or three days later. For her, these bitter-sweet occasions offered her an assurance that there was hope for the future. Her son continued to be in safe hands, perhaps then there was still hope for her husband's return.

My recollections of my days in the convent are very few, and what I do remember is the darkness of the spaces where I used to spend my days. Nor do I recall missing my parents or yearning for my previous life in our house in Salonica or even in Yiorgos and Elpida's home. I existed in a sort of psychological bubble; my expectations for an improvement in my condition muted, perhaps because of all the changes I had stumbled through in the preceding many months. I suppose that what mattered was the safety of everyday life, but I am unsure even of that. Did I know what it was to be safe or unsafe? After the war, on a few occasions I returned to the convent to visit Soeur Hélène and Soeur Anastasie, who had been my guardian in the convent. She, and a few other nuns, marveled that, while I was their guest in the convent, I did not show any desire to go out-of-doors, to play in the street, to escape from the confines of my new home. Life was proceeding on an even keel and that seemed to be good enough for me.

For my mother, the summer and autumn of 1943 were less agitated than the previous many months. Every now and then, she felt awkwardly, given the fact that the Fix estate had become a meeting place for German officers stationed in Athens. It was strange, she remembered more than once, serving them in the frequent receptions and dinner parties hosted by the Fixes. Fortunately, she was never singled out by Mrs. Fix, nor, certainly, was the young cook—she was not yet twenty-nine years old—invited to play the piano before guests.

As the autumn wore on and the weather began to change, the Fixes, following their habit, prepared to move from their summer estate in Neo Heraklion to their city home, which was, as my mother mentioned and I discovered much later from newspaper accounts of the Fix family, a large and elegant apartment in the very heart of Athens, a few paces away from the Royal (now the Presidential) Palace and the Royal (now the National) Garden. It was assumed that the staff would move with

COURAGE AND COMPASSION

the family, but a handful of employees would stay on to tend to the country estate. Summoning her courage, my mother approached Mr. Fix, who seemed to be overseeing the transfer, and asked if she could be among those to stay behind. Quite beyond being safer in the countryside, she imagined that, with the country home almost entirely empty, she might have the chance to take me with her, even if only for a few days at a time. Mr. Fix's refusal to grant her request initially puzzled my mother, although his reasons for keeping the second cook nearby are easily understood. Better to keep an eye on her and stop any mischief that might arise when she is out of sight.

So, sometime in late October or November, my mother, preceded by the Fix family, moved to one of the most elegant and comfortable streets in Athens. The Fix house was a stone's throw from the Royal Garden, where, on occasion, my mother would explore the beautiful tree-covered alleys and the goldfish ponds with the ducks scampering about. She often reminisced about these occasional outings, when, being close to nature, she felt more relaxed, even if not necessarily safer. You always had to be on the lookout to ensure that no one was following you or looking at you strangely. You always had to be alert, and this constant vigilance tired and worried her. But she did not give up her periodical strolls through the Garden. Being close to nature may also have been a pleasant reminder of the large garden in her family home, filled with fruit trees and flowers that she always loved. When, at long last, she was able to take me from my hideout and keep me to herself, the Garden was among the first places she took me. To this day, I have a soft spot for this Garden, for every time I walk through it, I remember my visits there with my mother in the summer and very early fall of 1944.

Now that they were in the center of town, perhaps to compensate for the family's refusal to let her stay on in the country, Mrs. Fix informed my mother that she was being promoted. Rather than continuing as a second cook, she would now become a house maid and spend most of her time in the house's reception area. This time, the adjustment was not hard. Tending to Mrs. Fix's needs proved to be not nearly as demanding as when she first arrived at the country estate. By now she had become accustomed to the uninterrupted pressures of the Fixes' social life. The need to prepare buffets and elaborate dinner tables, to meet Mrs. Fix's exacting standards, and to be always on call filled her days without allowing her much time to worry. And so it went from mid-autumn 1943 to mid-winter 1944. Until January, my mother continued her regular visits to the convent. Only now, the distance between the Fix apartment and my hideout was only about half of what it had been before. During her short stopovers at the convent, she had a chance to see me from distance and occasionally bring Soeur Hélène up to date.

The seeming tranquility and orderliness of conditions in the Fix household were in sharp contrast with the tragic situation in the country, especially in the streets of Athens. Food shortages were so acute that people were, literally, dying of hunger, their bodies even abandoned in the streets. Anger at the German occupiers was growing, and the ranks of the resistance were being swollen by citizens, exasperated both by the lack of adequate food and by the seeming indifference and incompetence of the various Greek governments—both in the country and in exile—to address the problems of provisioning and safety. In the meantime, the Germans had now transported to concentration camps and there murdered the vast majority of Salonica's Jews. But their fiendish policy continued unabated in other parts of Greece where Jews were rounded up and sent to their deaths. Homes were searched for suspicious inhabitants, Jews and members of the resistance were singled out by some Greeks eager to gain advantage with the occupying forces, a sense of uncertainty and precariousness was widespread.

Perhaps because of the pervasive fear generated by these conditions or perhaps because of other, more specific reasons unknown to my mother, Mrs. Fix spoke to her one day in February or March (my mother did not remember the exact date) and informed her that unfortunately she had to leave. No other explanation was offered—simply it was unwise for her to stay on, however pleased they were with her work. Obviously, the risk for the Fixes—not to mention for my mother—was too great. What if one of the house staff let slip a word too many or a German officer suspected something or, worse yet, a Greek collaborator, of whom any number were around at the Fixes' social gatherings, asked a question or two? It was one thing to want to be helpful, altogether a different matter to run unnecessary risks, for which the punishment would be exemplary. Soon after her conversation with Mrs. Fix, Mr. Fix himself spoke to her and offered to help by presenting her with a choice. She could, of course, leave and be on her own, or if she preferred, she could move to the home of a sister-in-law of the Fixes, who needed household help. Of course, the second option was safer, and she took it.

In the next two months or so, my mother worked for two different families. First, there was a short stint at the Fixes' sister-in-law, where, for unclear reasons, she stayed for a short time only. Then, she moved to the home of the Tzatos family, themselves refugees from Xanthi, in northeastern Greece, whom, in later years, she remembered with great affection. There were five of them, Mr. Tzatos, his wife and mother-in-law, and their two small children, a boy and a girl. All together they shared a three-bedroom apartment, my mother sleeping in a room with the mother-in-law. I think I understand the reason for my mother's satisfaction with her new situation. Rather than having to clean or to cook, her principal responsibility now was staying with the children, helping them with their lessons, and teaching them French and Spanish. The Tzatos turned out to have been kind and did not prod about her background. Mr. Tzatos, himself, chose to sit in on the children's language lessons—ostensibly to learn the languages, but, in all likelihood, to keep an eye on the newcomer's behavior and ensure that nothing strange was said during the children's lessons. However pleasant and quiet things were in the Tzatos home, soon the outside world intruded in the family's quiet routine. One evening, the older lady with whom my mother shared a room, asked my mother a question or two about her background, why it was that such a well-educated person found herself alone and jobless in the middle of wartime Athens. The conversation was not tense, nor did it lead to any particular conclusion, but a few days later Mr. Tzatos had a private exchange with my mother. The family liked her very much, they were especially grateful for her good relations with the children, but times were very difficult. It was too dangerous for Mrs. Eleni to continue staying with them in their home. He suggested that my mother move to an apartment nearby, where she would be responsible for her safety, and, if she wanted, she could continue giving lessons to the children a few hours a day.

Thus, in no more than a couple of months, my mother found herself changing homes three times. It was strange, she thought, that nothing exceptional had happened to precipitate these changes, that she had become a twentieth-century version of the wandering Jew in a quiet, routine sort of manner—only after moving to the United States did my teenaged daughter correct her, "wandering Jewess, Nana, this is how we say it in this country." The Fixes, their in-laws, and now the Tzatos all seemed to be accommodating, kind, even generous people. No trace of antisemitism, or of any other prejudice, colored their behavior. But in those times, even kind and selfless people were driven to think of the dangers to which they and their families were exposed if they sheltered someone like my mother. Not the banality of evil, to draw on an expression of one of the major political theorists of the twentieth century—rather, the banality of goodness. More often than not, a decent person chooses to help not because of a heroic instinct or a wish to do something out of the ordinary or because of a powerful ethical imperative. Decency calls you to help if you can accommodate your action into your daily habits and routines. But when your help threatens to compromise your safety and the well-being of those close to you, you stop and think twice and, more often than not, step back and place a distance between your world and that of the one in need of help. There were a lot of decent people in Greece during the country's occupation by Germany. In the course of my family's adventures during the early 1940s, we encountered two persons who, justifiably, could be called heroes. They were Mrs. Fani Kalkou and Soeur Hélène Capart, who, for years after the war, shared with my mother her memories of the German occupation. As she wrote to my mother, shortly after my father's death: "Notre vie a été liée à la vôtre pendant les mauvais jours." To which my mother might well have answered: "Pas seulement."

And yet ... Reading some of Soeur Hélène's letters to my mother when we were already in Cleveland, I came across one, written on 24 April 1967, that startled me. I had not expected our family heroine to whom we owe our survival to say something so different from what, no doubt uncritically, I would have anticipated from her. The letter was written three days after the Colonels' coup against the country's democratic government. Of course, no one could have yet imagined the horrors that the military junta would perpetrate in the following seven years. But from the moment of the coup, an outcry had arisen in Greece itself and in much of Europe and elsewhere. To those of us who protested, it seemed barbaric that a military dictatorship could have been imposed in a European country more than twenty years after World War II. Yet, to my astonishment, Soeur Hélène did not appear to be dissatisfied at the violent turn political life had taken in Greece. "En ces jours de Paques où la situation gouvernementale vient de se modifier—pour un grand bien j'en suis sure . . ." Even the greatest of heroes have their weaknesses. Why should Soeur Hélène not have hers?

6.

In the Labyrinth

A fuzzy memory of that night lingers on in my mind. I am sleeping deeply, covered in my blankets to keep the intense cold away. The shuffling of feet reaches me in my sleeping state. Unexpectedly, Soeur Anastasie first gently, then urgently shakes me and tells me to wake up. I try to open my eyes, but darkness envelops everything around me. I am helped out of bed and quickly dressed. I ask no questions, and no explanations are offered. One quick and abrupt gesture follows another until I am ready to follow instructions. All the while Soeur Anastasie, familiar and trustworthy, holds my hand, another nun picks me up, holds me tight, and someone covers me from head to toe in one of my blankets. I do not resist, nor do I protest. I trust the nuns and see no reason to suspect that anything strange might happen. Quickly, a dream-like procession—the two nuns and half-sleeping me—moves toward one of the nunnery's back exits. We walk for a few (or is it many?) minutes in the street, where the cold makes itself felt, and enter a house where some children and a woman—neither young nor old—quickly greet us. I look around and see a greater number of children than I remember ever seeing before. The oldest boy of the group, I discover later he is more than half a dozen years older than me, picks me up from the nun's arms and sets me down softly. The surroundings are new to me, as are the faces. No one is saying much of anything, the children make no noise, the older lady, who seems to be their mother, smiles but makes no effort to touch me. At a certain point, looking around me, I realize that the two nuns are gone, probably having quickly retreated to the nunnery. I must have looked dazed, unsure of what was going on, but I do not cry or protest. A small tin cup with milk is handed to me; I suspect I drank it. The air of urgency—of imminent danger—is only half clear to me. I had first left my home about nine months before—long enough to become accustomed to the succession of quick, sharp changes in my life but short enough to become aware that, as my youngest daughter might say today, this was my "new normal."

So began a new stage of my life, from about December 1943 to about May–June 1944. Today, as I am writing these lines, I am fast slipping toward my eighty-second birthday, and five or six months seem like a flash that passes in a moment. At this age, you blink, and the months are gone! When you are a kid, six months seem like an eternity—months are endless, summers stretch out forever, a school year unfolds around you (or perhaps is it inside your head?) at an almost imperceptible pace. In my old age, I am struck repeatedly by the tricks played by time. Our flight from home at the time of the German Occupation, and everything that followed—during that earth-shattering set of events known as the Shoah—began and finished in a period of less than two years. The annihilation of Salonica's Jewish community was consummated in a mere six months—less than it takes for a baby to be born from the moment of its conception. At the time of my latest midnight flight in December 1943, I do not recall remembering my other recent adventures. Or if

I did, I did not dwell on them. They were part of a long-past experience. They had begun on 21 March 1943, and now we were in early December.

The beginning of this string of adventures did not seem in my mind to be connected to my later ones. Life for me, then, as perhaps is the case for any child that age, was a series of staccato happenings, one following another. I suspect that a sediment of those other experiences had settled somewhere in my subconscious. Yet, like the remains of a bottle of bad wine, they lay inert where they had been deposited. Only later, when I grew older did I think of all these events—from the time of *Mamà* Elpida, to that of Mrs. Kalkou, and of *Yiayià* (grandma) Harikleia, whom we shall meet below—as bits of one slowly unfolding story, which today, so many years later, seems to have been governed by an inexorable dynamic. Only after having left my new home was I told what had happened that night, and why I was rushed from the nunnery. (Years later, while visiting the convent, one of the nuns, but I do not recall which one, who had witnessed my escape said that I had left like a thief in the night! Nice compliment, I thought. If only I had known that this was a biblical citation from Saint Paul's first letter to Thessalonians, a fact pointed out to me recently by a generous friend much better versed in the texts of the New Testament than I am! I suspect the nun was perfectly well aware of the text's origin, but I dare not imagine what she had intended by making this comment.) Soeur Hélène had found out that the authorities (unclear if the Germans or the Greek police) had been tipped off that a Jewish boy was hidden in the convent. In anticipation of a police raid, the Mother Superior discussed the matter with some of the nuns and decided that I should be transferred to another location. A safe refuge had already been agreed upon, and, in the middle of that night, I was carried to Mrs. Kalkou's house. For the following five or six months I lived with her family, which, for me, for all the hardships of those months, was something of an unexpectedly pleasant interlude.

Since March when I had been taken to Elpida and Yiorgos's home, I was not in contact with a single child. My life had been solitary, either isolated in my hosts' home, and later in the convent, or I had been carefully hidden during the train ride from Salonica to Athens. Tony had been deprived of play time, and that is why he has become such a serious boy, my mother used to say when I attended elementary school, starting in the autumn of 1945. It is not that before leaving our house on Evzonon Street I had been overwhelmed with playmates. But there were children in the street, and one of them, living next door, had been within eyesight whenever I would drift to our house's back terrace. I suspect there must have been other children in the vicinity, but I do not remember them. In any case, I had not been deprived of toys, brought in abundance to our home by grandparents, uncles, aunts, neighbors, and Molho and Alkalay family friends. Had I shared these toys with other children, or did I mostly play with them alone? I can't remember. However sociable I had been with other children, and however happily adjusted a child I may have been, the months immediately before arriving at the Kalkou home had been a prolonged period of isolation, a near quarantine.

Now, for the first time in more than half a year, I was surrounded by children. There were five of them, ranging in age from those substantially older than me to some who were a couple of years beyond my age. It was in that environment that I learned to socialize with children. In one sense I was even luckier than one might expect. None of the five children had my name. I could continue being called Antonis or Antonakis without having to undergo a name change. The sheer chance of bearing Dr. Vaïnanidis's name had given me an advantage during the first months of my vagabondage after March 1943. Now, my name was simply added the collection of names of the Kalkou children. We played and ran around, but also, as I recall, we spent periods of just sitting alone in a corner and passing the time away. I also began the slow process of learning about sharing and giving precedence to others. I think that I learned by observing, without being given lessons of proper behavior. However vague my recollections of those months, I do not remember any pushing or screaming. Now, it appears to me that an air of urgency hung over "our" home, and it regulated the cadences of daily life. Of course, I do not remember everything.

But some things I remember all too well. Above all, I remember the cold and the hunger. The cold was intense. Not only out of doors but also in the house. It turns out that the winter of 1943–44 was one of the coldest on record. I do not remember how we tried to heat the house. We probably didn't. You just wore all your sweaters and coats, covered yourself in a blanket, and shivered away during the day. As far as I remember, no one got sick—no sniffles, coughs, or fevers. Were we stronger then than we are now? Perhaps. Then, there was the hunger. Food was really scarce. It is not that there were insufficient quantities of food. There were times when almost no food at all was available. I remember we all lined up and each of us would be given one big slice of bread and our tin cup full of water. This was our ration for the day. Another piece of bread and another tin cup full of water would have to wait for the next day. You had to make do with your ration, however hungry you were. Boys or girls, older or younger, native to the family or a guest such as I was—we were all entitled to the same amount of food: very little of it. I do not remember complaints, even though, obviously, we were all hungry. In retrospect, what strikes me now is the equality of all the children. Mrs. Kalkou made no distinctions. This sort of spartan fairness has stayed with me as an abiding memory of those days; an equality of suffering, or, as some of my colleagues might say today, an equality of opportunity that contributed to binding us into a group, perhaps giving us a sense of community. January and February were spent being very cold and very hungry. Did we suffer? Of course, we did. We ate very little, and it showed. By the time I left Mrs. Kalkou's home, I was thin as a reed. But so were the other children. In my case I was so thin my cheek bones began protruding from my face, just as, more recently, I have seen pictures of small children in very poor parts of the world. I do recall repeatedly touching my cheekbone and wondering if it would continue sticking out of my face. It was a prospect that worried me.

I remember something else vividly from those days: the church and my regular attendance of church services. The Kalkous were a religious and observant family. They belonged to the Uniate Church, a confession of Christianity that, while adhering to the Roman Catholic Church and thus acknowledging papal supremacy, maintained its own, Christian Orthodox rites. Normally, on holidays or on Sundays, adherents to the Uniate Church attended regular Greek Orthodox churches. This is what we did. Our attendance was regular, and I became fascinated with the ritual that had also drawn me while I was at the convent. I was too young to be in some way indoctrinated, but I was often invited to discharge responsibilities of an altar boy. The priest of the church we frequented seemed to have taken a liking to me, and Mrs. Kalkou, so as not to arouse any suspicions about her newly appeared "nephew," did not discourage his invitation to have me assist him while he celebrated Mass. Although I do not remember many details of my regular involvement in the rituals, there is one incident which left a deep imprint in my mind.

It was Easter Sunday, which, I recently discovered by consulting Google, happened to be on 23 April 1944, a sunny, warm day as I remember it. The Mass was finished, the faithful had gathered in the yard in front of the church chatting with each other, the priest, wearing his ritual garb also slowly emerged from the church, accompanied by his favorite altar boy. Despite the times, there was a happy atmosphere in the crowd, everyone more or less cheerful at the joyfulness of the occasion, hoping, no doubt, that the Resurrection celebrated by Christianity would be followed by the country's rise from its miserable condition. I stood next to the priest and took in the scene, smiling at anyone willing to look at me. Unexpectedly, in the midst of the crowd, a lady, vaguely familiar to me, appeared. Her drab clothes were matched by her serious mien; she seemed to be alone and not to know anyone. Slowly she made her way through the crowd and approached the priest. She looked at me persistently, but I continued not to recognize her, or perhaps I did not wish to recognize her. She came next to the priest, kissed his hand, and asked him if the little boy standing next to him was good and if he followed his instructions. He is excellent, said the priest. And turning to me he asked: "Tell this nice lady what you want to become when you grow up." Without a moment's hesitation, I answered that when I grew up, I would become the Archbishop of Athens. The priest, satisfied with my answer, smiled to the lady, and patted me on the head. Later, many years later, I thought that it is always best to get great ambitions of this sort out of your system when you are a child. This, certainly, has been the case with me.

My mother slowly backed into the crowd, and I lost sight of her. Whenever in later years she and I talked about this incident, she would almost always mutter, "If only the priest had known my secret, where would we be now?" To which I would teasingly respond that it was a good thing I did not recognize her. And if she showed some irritation at my response, I would continue by asking her if she was sure that the priest did not know her secret. Could this have been a possibility? I wonder.

In the months I spent in the Kalkou household, my mother, having left the Fixes and the two other families for whom she had worked briefly, was able to improve her situation. All along, Soeur Hélène had been on the lookout for places where her ward could hide more safely, and where, sometime in the future, she could be reunited with her son. In the end, thanks to my mother's excellent knowledge of languages (in addition to her command of Greek, she was entirely fluent in French and English, and her Spanish, because of our family's use of Ladino, was more than passable), a position was found for her as an assistant with the International Red Cross in Athens, which was administered by the office of the Swiss Red Cross (Joint Relief Committee for Greece. International Red Cross.) For my mother, this was a great improvement. Now she could count on regular pay, although very often she was paid in kind—once a month she was entitled to a box full of food, selected by the officers of the Red Cross. Then, thanks to this new position, she managed to find new lodgings—the rent was two liters of olive oil a month.

Her new house was a small and unpretentious one-story but welcoming building at 12 Vizyinou Street in Patissia. It was

COURAGE AND COMPASSION

in a modest, middle-class neighborhood, about a fifteen- to twenty-minute walk from the convent and from Mrs. Kalkou's house, a block away from Papadiamantis Square, then as now a large and well-tended oasis of green. The owners, an older lady (who, for me, became *Yiayià* Harikleia) and her daughter, "Aunt" Foffi, who must have been a little older than my mother, were willing to share it with us. Recently, for the first time in almost seventy-five years, I took a stroll to that neighborhood. The house, largely fixed up or built entirely anew according to what a neighbor told me, is abandoned, with a sadly faded "For Sale" sign stuck to the front door. The neighbor did not know the owners nor did his memory extend to the years immediately after the war, when the wartime tenants presumably continued to live in it. Seeing the house in a street I certainly did not recognize evoked contradictory feelings. I knew I had lived there for almost a year in unusual circumstances. I should have felt a sense of familiarity. But I had to force myself to rouse up an emotion at its sight. So much time had passed. So many memories had vanished. Sentiments had changed. Was the person standing on the sidewalk staring at the house today the same person who had lived in it decades ago? I remember one detail of the house that I knew nearly three-quarters of a century ago: the side entrance to the garden, through a narrow, tiled, open-aired corridor that led to the house's principal door, and behind it, to the wider and larger garden. In the early 1940s, an iron gate closed off this corridor from the street. That was an important consideration in my mother's choice of this house, because she was already thinking of ways to take me and have me live with her. Fencing me in the grounds of the house was important, but as she soon discovered, her plans to keep me enclosed and isolated from the surrounding world did not work as she had expected. Today, the corridor has been incorporated into the house, while the garden, if it still exists, is not visible from the street.

Once lodgings were found, the next task was to ensure that adequate food be put on the table, not necessarily for her but for me. Finding food in wartime Athens was a major, often insurmountable problem. If you could pay in hard currency, or gold pounds, you could almost certainly procure the necessary for your family. But how many people could do that? The vast majority of the population was often on the verge of starvation. The black market in food stuffs was thriving in Athens. After the war horrible stories were recounted, of desperate people exchanging entire apartments in Athens for a few large containers of olive oil. At the Kalkous's, we were not starving probably because bits of food were passed over to the house from the convent, which itself occasionally procured it from the islands where the majority of the nuns still had families. Quite simply, we were nearly always hungry. However extreme such situations, the fact is that my mother could not decide to get me back with her until she had some assurance that she could feed me at home. A few weeks after starting at the Red Cross, the Director agreed to my mother's request that I, also, be listed as being an employee of the organization. I could thus be entitled to a daily ration of food. The necessary for survival had been secured, and a next step could now be taken. The Red Cross records should show that in the summer of 1944 a new employee, named Tony (or perhaps Tonis or Antonis) Molho, was added to the roll of people working for it!

By then, both she and Soeur Hélène had revealed to the Director of the Red Cross office the secret for my mother's condition in Athens: a highly educated woman with middle-class manners and excellent command of several languages, living alone in Athens, her husband having disappeared almost a year before, and her son being in the custody of a widow in another part of town. What might account for this woman's condition? There were two likely answers: Either she was a communist or she was Jewish. In either case she would have to hide. In her case, Soeur Hélène's mediation rather excluded, although perhaps not entirely, the possibility that she was a communist. The most likely answer was that Mrs. Eleni was Jewish. The secret was now out of the bag. Of course, all the while Athens remained under German occupation, it was extremely dangerous to be identified as Jewish—even more foolish to declare yourself a Jew. At the time of D-day (6 June 1944), my mother was at the Red Cross. Later, she remembered that day very well. While she was at the office, she received a triumphant telephone call from her previous employer, Mr. Tzatos, telling her that everyone's suffering was about to finish. The American armies had landed in Europe! The news had come from the secret BBC news program that Mr. Tzatos, like many Greeks, were in the habit of listening to secretly in their homes.

As I am recalling and trying to write down some of these memories, one thing is becoming increasingly clear in my mind. A little more than a year following my parents' escape from home, slowly and after great uncertainty, my mother was beginning to get a little greater control of her life. The same could also be most probably said about my father. But in his case, the lack of information about his experience in the resistance makes it difficult to draw a picture of his condition. The fact that he survived surely means something. But I do not know what it took for him to survive. Was he accepted by his comrades for what he was, a Jew trying to escape the Nazis? Were some men and women in his unit especially helpful, or, contrarily, were there others who threw up obstacles in his attempt to survive? To what extent was his Jewishness a factor in his dealings with his comrades? I have no answers.

In the case of my mother, I know enough to realize that step by step, month after month, she managed to set her feet a little more securely on the ground, to feel that some greater predictability governed her daily existence. Of course, at any moment, the roof could have caved in. After the war, she recounted to me the experiences of a number of Jews she knew, most of them from Salonica but hiding in Athens, who, as late as August 1944, were caught and deported to and murdered in concentration camps. For my mother, but not only for her, chronology here was important. By August 1944, it was clear that the Nazi regime was tottering, that the odds against German armies were increasingly stacking up in their disfavor. Still, even though time was running out on them, their determination to exterminate Jews—all the Jews they could get their hands on—remained undiminished. How to explain this visceral hatred? How could one forgive them? These questions obsessed her in the years after the war. I recall her telling me when I was a little older, and had begun to understand the dimension of the tragedy, the story of a small number, really a handful, of Jews who had managed to hide in Salonica during the war. They were discovered by the Germans a day or two before their troops finally withdrew from the city. Even so, they were dragged out of their hiding places, lined up against a wall and executed.

But in her case, and by extension in mine, a human chain of individuals who mostly did not know each other and had not coordinated their actions, stepped in and offered sustenance and refuge. From Soeur Hélène to the nuns in the convent, none of whom betrayed our secret, to the Fixes and their household help, to Mrs. Kalkou and her children, and now *Yiayià* Harikleia and her daughter Foffi, all together had woven a sort of protective wall around my mother and succeeded day by day to keep her out of harm's way. The rings of this cordon sanitaire were strong enough to hold even in the most difficult times, when turning a Jew (woman or small child) to the authorities might have seemed profitable and advantageous.

After a little more than six months at the Kalkou household, I left sometime in June 1944, and began a not always easy cohabitation with my mother at 12 Vizyinou Street. We stayed there for a little less than one year, until April 1945. In recent months, I was curious to find more about the details of the transfer, even the exact dates, so I called the current offices of the Red Cross in Athens about their wartime archives. Predictably, I was told that they did not think there were any "such old" documents in their offices. The only evidence I have is my mother's very precious Red Cross ID. Despite its miserable state of preservation, it provides some evidence, which is at once revealing if not always easy to interpret. One thing is clear: the information on this ID shows that at the Red Cross, it was almost certainly known that "Lily Molhou," daughter of Nissim Alkalay, born in 1916, was Jewish. Evidently, there are a couple of strange details in the registration of her name. They make me wonder about her thinking. Her surname is made to sound Greek, Molho given in the genitive (or possessive) form as Molhou, as if the name had a Greek origin, and could be declined in more than one case. But this almost never happens in Spanish. As far as I can tell, my mother never used, either before or after, this Hellenized genitive form of her surname. Molhou is written in her own handwriting both in the English and Greek sides of the ID card which means that she herself had chosen (or had, perhaps, been urged) to change slightly her surname. Then, there is her birthdate, here listed (again, in her handwriting) as 1916, making her appear one year younger. Why these two changes? The Hellenization of her surname is more mysterious: Might she spontaneously have wished to appear more Greek than her father's unmistakably Jewish name indicated? I never asked her, as I discovered this Red Cross ID among a stack of seemingly unimportant papers, years after her death. And why did she change the year of her birth? The only possible explanation is that she did not want to appear to have reached her thirtieth birthday so soon after taking up her position at the Red Cross. But why?

In any case, sometime in June with a paying position secured and decent lodgings also found, it was time to put into action her plan to bring me back into the family fold. At some point, I accompanied my mother to our new dwelling. For me, this was another major transition. Once again, I remember nothing about my move to Vizyinou Street. Did I resist this new change? How did I accept leaving "my home" to which I had become accustomed and accept my mother's company, who, just a few weeks earlier, had appeared to be an unknown person to me? Did I miss the company of the Kalkou children? Was the departure accompanied by farewell hugs, and promises to meet again soon? Was I hesitant or suspicious of our new landladies? And what about Victor, our new next-door neighbors' dog? When did I first meet him? None of these details has stayed with me, although with time I grew increasingly attached to Victor, who became a pleasant companion and playmate. Around the corner from us, there was a parrot who spent his days sitting in a big cage on the porch of a rather nice large house, whistling its time away. But with only slight encouragement, it would launch into a well-known anti-Italian, anti-Mussolini song, probably learned from its owners around October 1940 when Italy invaded Greece. By the time we moved to our house, having the parrot sing out of doors the song about "Mussolini You're a Fool" was not exactly acceptable entertainment. I was told that if ever I would be outside and close to this singing bird, I should never goad it to sing. I did not understand the importance of this prohibition, and more than once the bird's owner showed up in his house's front door, shaking his hand in exasperation at my lack of discipline and my inability to contain my pleasure at hearing this marvelous bird sing. One of my first great pleasures following my father's return was to lead him, holding him by the hand, to the parrot and urging it to show us its singing prowess. By then, the Germans had withdrawn, and the parrot was finally free to sing. But that first time in my father's presence, the bird stayed mute! I was disconsolate, but my father, always eager to find ways to make me feel better, ventured the thought that that morning the parrot probably suffered from a stomachache. Once it got better, it would no doubt sing again. Indeed, this is what happened. One of the reasons I got along with my father, almost immediately after his return home, was his accurate prediction of the parrot's behavior.

For all the fuzziness of the first impressions, I have a clear recollection of the house. My mother and I shared a room with a nice window. I was allowed to roam through the house and in the garden, with one exception: the formal living room, which was nicely furnished and at whose center was an upright piano, which the younger of the two landladies played almost every day. I was told in no uncertain terms I could not even dream of touching it. I have fond memories of the garden, whose two or three tall trees provided welcome shade in the summer months. Perhaps the part of the house I enjoyed most was the long corridor, inside the iron gate, that led, as you entered, on the right to the house entrance, and further down to the garden. For some reason, I spent hours playing in this corridor. Soon after moving to this new house, one of my father's brothers, Uncle Isaac (known then as Uncle Yannis) began coming once a week to see me, also to ensure that I was well. Uncle Yannis and Uncle Raphael/Nicos had found work in a warehouse operated by the Red Cross where daily arrivals and shipments of consignments were noted in chalk on a blackboard. I have no idea about the availability of chalk in wartime Athens, but the fact is that every time my uncle visited me, he brought me one or two small pieces of chalk. These small presents gave me great joy, and I remember awaiting them with much anticipation. I used to play with the chalk in the outside corridor, scribbling on the tiles and drawing large designs of the sort small children draw.

One of my very pleasant memories of those months was related to the warehouse where my uncles had found employment. Sometime in August or September of 1944 my mother took me along to visit her two brothers-in-law at their place of work. While we were there, Uncle Yannis read out a letter he had recently received from his brother, Uncle Maurice, who was in Africa. The letter announced my cousin Robert's birth, a little more than a year before, in June 1943. My two uncles present on the occasion cheered, smiled at me, and hugged me, explaining that now I had a cousin. I had no idea what that meant, but over the years Robert became a very close friend, and his recent death deeply saddened me. He was the first of my generation of Molho cousins to have been born free. During his life, his intense intellectual curiosity, his cheerfulness and pleasant disposition remain vivid in my memory, always related to the semi-darkness of a basement warehouse where I first discovered that I had acquired a cousin.

For me, one of the most memorable events of those days took place on 12 July, my fifth birthday, very shortly after my arrival at this new house. My mother got home from work earlier than usual. After her return, all of us, our two land ladies and I, were summoned by my mother to the formal living room, which was ordinarily out of bounds for me, and invited to sit down. I remember resisting the invitation because it was a nice summer day, and I was playing in the garden. Finally, I went in, and saw the three ladies sitting in a semi-circle. All of them, one more anxiously than the other, kept telling me to look around and find something interesting. What was it? I made the rounds of the room. Nothing! Keep looking, everyone encouraged me. The warning never to touch the piano had sunk in. I stayed clear of the piano even though from the corner of an eye I had spotted a curious object propped up on the keyboard. Finally, *Yiayià* Harikleia got up, took me by the hand and led me to the piano. How exciting, I thought! I had never even gotten close to the piano. Now, I would be allowed to play with the white and black keys, just as the younger of the two hostesses did when she practiced. But no! The surprise was different. It was not my proximity to the piano. Rather, it was the object that had been propped up against the keyboard. I was befuddled. What was this square object, with a nice bright cover? At long last, the mystery was solved. I picked it up, tore the cover and was confronted by a brown square object. The ladies kept up with their encouragements. Try it, they shouted all together. This time my mother came over, she cut off a piece of the chocolate, and told me to taste it. Good, I thought! This chocolate, brought home by my mother from the Red Cross, was indeed good. That was the first step in my rediscovery of tastes that I had simply forgotten. Ice cream came only about a year later, in the summer of 1945, when we were again in Salonica. My mother's very close friend, the strikingly beautiful Mrs. Eliza Arouh, who had returned from Auschwitz, took me to have my first taste of ice cream at the well-known pastry shop Hatzis. That befuddled me even more than the chocolate. No sooner had I very hesitantly put in my mouth a small spoonful of ice cream than, to the endless amusement of waiters and customers sitting nearby, I began blowing on it, fearing that it was so hot I would burn my tongue!

The days and weeks went by at the house on Vizyinou Street. I spent my time mostly playing by myself, in the garden and the corridor. As time went on, I became familiar with the two landladies, one of whom I called grandma, the other aunt. Occasionally, accompanied either by my mother or one of the two ladies, I would walk in the streets around the house, trying each time to ensure that we passed by the parrot's house. I think that I had become well accustomed to the immediate neighborhood, and I remember the small grocery store a few blocks away. I also knew exactly where Papadiamantis Square was, a few minutes' walk from the house. It always seemed like an attractive place to visit, although I do not remember being taken to it often. At a certain point, it must have been in August or September, before the Germans had retreated from Athens, my mother began occasionally taking me to her work with her. This, I confess, was not very smart of her, because, as we discovered one morning, it was dangerous to do so. But the change of scenery pleased me; even the prospect of idling away for a whole day in the office did not bother me much. I was not used to having my days filled with excitement.

The trip to the office one morning provided more than enough excitement. As usual, we walked to the stop and got on the first tram that came by. I held on to my mother's hand, and she led me to the space behind the back door. The tram was full, no one paying much attention to the other passengers. Then, all of a sudden, I became aware of a big commotion when, at one of the subsequent stops, two men entered the tram, one from the front door, the other from the back. The sight of those two men had an immediate effect on everyone, many passengers became agitated, as the two newcomers, policemen in civil clothes, proceeded to move, one in the direction of the other, asking each passenger for his papers. They seemed to have spotted someone suspicious, and the two converged to the point where this poor man was standing. A big commotion ensued, the policemen trying to arrest the passenger, other passengers arguing with the policemen, the suspect first arguing, then physically resisting. At the height of this confusion, whether by design or accident, the tram stopped and its doors were opened. My mother later thought that the conductor, by opening the doors, had wanted to complicate the policemen's work.

No sooner had the doors opened than my mother hurriedly led me up to a man, took my hand and placed it in his. Unobserved by the policemen, she then jumped off the tram. It all happened in a few seconds. The tram started in its way, myself frozen in astonishment, fortunately not crying or protesting. I must have wondered something. But I cannot remember what. Instinctively I followed my protector. He held my hand, and we slowly moved toward the back door. At the next stop, he nudged me to get off the tram, together with him. The two of us, I holding his hand, without a word being exchanged between us, started retracing the tram's itinerary, toward the stop where my mother had escaped. Sure enough, a few minutes later, I saw her moving fast in our direction. Not many words were exchanged between her and the unknown man. All the while I clung to my mother's dress, she spoke with him excitedly, the *deus ex machina* said something I don't remember, he smiled, patted me on the head, and went on his way.

That stranger had provided the cover that helped my mother squeeze through a potentially disastrous run-in with the police. Now, whenever this incident comes back to mind, I am close to overwhelmed by the thought of the improbable coincidences that governed that moment. What got into my mother to entrust me to a man whom she had never met before? She had always been and would continue to be a strong and decisive person. She knew her mind and, if she had to, could make crucial decisions at the drop of a hat. Her cheek in deciding, in a split second, to hand me to a complete stranger leaves me speechless. What if this man had simply turned me over to the police? He could have easily said: "Here is an abandoned child. Why don't you figure out what you want to do with him?" Just as easily he could have walked away with me, kept me for his family. How did my mother instinctively know that he would choose not to do this? As best as I can remember, no words were exchanged between them. Might it be that a lightning-fast, silent communication between them—a nod of the head, a wink, or a firm glance—had cleared the way for what happened? Perhaps. Even so, how was it that this unknown man reflexively understood the need to step forth and take the risk that many others would have simply shied away from, assuming even that they would have understood what was at stake? Without much of a fuss, he did what he thought was right. I do not have a convincing explanation. Whenever I think back to that unknown man's gesture, I am led to think that his was one way of expressing his opposition to the occupation authorities governing the country. Massive demonstrations against the Germans and their collaborationist Greek stooges had taken place not that long before, most impressively the crowds that had gathered at the funeral of Kostis Palamas, the poet who, before a crowd of as many one hundred thousand people, had been eulogized by another poet, Angelos Sikelianos. A sort of visceral opposition to the country's occupiers had penetrated Greek society, down to a capillary level. The unknown passenger in the tram that summer of 1944 may have simply wanted to express his sense of shared destiny and solidarity for my mother, who by her desire to evade the hated secret police, had marked herself as someone not in the state's good graces.

My mother and I walked the rest of the way to her office. It was very close to the center of town, not a great distance from where we had met following our respective improvised descents from the tram. Every time I walk on my way to the Gennadeios Library, where in recent years I have spent many pleasant hours exploring its wonderful collection of books, I think of this incident. It is a stone's throw from where the offices of the International Red Cross were located during the war.

In thinking of, or perhaps imagining, the motives of this incident's protagonist, almost certainly I have been influenced by a memory of mine, altogether real and clearly imprinted on my mind. Shortly after the war, when my father had reopened his store in Salonica, at Kapodistriou Street, no. 2, on occasion, just as darkness was beginning to envelop the city, a man (not always the same man) would slink along the side street around the corner from our store, looking for a place to hide. Those were the days when the civil war had begun to convulse Greek society, and real or suspected "leftists" were pitilessly hunted down by the Security Police. Whenever my father spotted one of these people, he waited for the clerks to leave for the day, then quietly gestured in the suspect's direction, opened the store entrance, bade him in, then drew down the metal rolls, lifted a hard to spot opening that led to the store basement, and invited the man to venture down. The secret opening was closed, one of the big tables on which merchandise would be shown to clients was moved to cover the opening, my father locked up the store and went home. The next morning, he would leave the house very early, a little before dawn, returned to the store, and let his frightened guest out. Not many words were exchanged between them; nothing compelled my father to offer shelter to someone who was being hunted down. I suspect it was his own memory of the help given to him by the Greek Resistance, and the moral debt he nurtured for the rest of his life toward the men and women who had stood by him. He never boasted about this, even when, to do so in the United States, would have been relatively safe. You do things because of a moral obligation, not because you want to be recognized for your actions by your friends and relatives. This is a lesson he tried to pass on to me and to my sister. I was myself witness to at least two of his quiet and effective actions, but I know for a fact that this silent ritual took place several more times. Nothing was said at home (at least not within my earshot) about the refuge offered to these men of the underground.

    I am unsure about the similarity between the two acts of solidarity I just described. In the case of my father, as I just mentioned, there was a debt of gratitude and an honor-bound obligation that almost certainly led him to do something that was risky and potentially dangerous. I have no idea what drove the anonymous man in the tram to act as he did. I doubt that religious conviction, an ethic rooted in Christian morality, might have inspired him. But here I may simply be expressing my own anti-religious prejudice that my gratitude to Soeur Hélène and Mrs. Kalkou should have mitigated. Otherwise, I confess to having only one explanation: Honor, or as the almost untranslatable Greek term would have it, φιλότιμο, love of one's own honor and the imperative to shield it from dishonorable and petty actions. Simple self-respect.

7.
A Yearning for Home

By early October 1944, the German occupation of Greece was coming to an end. The Soviet armies had begun to batter the Germans, and the Oberkommando decided to pull its forces out of Greece and reinforce, as best they could, their armies on the Eastern front. Soon, my father made his way to Athens from the Underground; shortly thereafter, he would return to Salonica to pick up the pieces of his business and to prepare for the return of my mother and me to our home while we, within a few months, also returned to Salonica while the Civil War had engulfed Greece. All this happened within a short period—from mid-October 1944 to mid-April 1945. By the end of that April my parents' *nostos*, their longing for home, had been fulfilled. All along, their Ithaca had been Salonica. Until they actually got back to the land of their origins, they did not waver for a moment from their desire to reconnect with their roots and refashion their lives as they remembered them. Some other Jews from Salonica, especially those who survived the concentration camp infernos, did not even bother to return to their old homes but moved directly to Palestine or to other European havens. Interestingly, many of them did not even once, following resettlement in their new homes, return to their old

Heimat. Not so my parents or my two uncles who had lived through the war in Athens. In their minds, their home could not have been anywhere but in Salonica. The *douceur de vie* that generations of middle-class Salonican Jews had cherished remained deeply ingrained in their consciousness. If only they had known...

All this is clear in retrospect. Not until later, after the war and the slow reconstruction of daily life, did the fragments of our wartime adventures add up to a cohesive, integrated story. My parents and others in their condition lived, breathless as it were, to survive, intent only upon getting through. Almost immediately following our return to Salonica, parents, close relatives, and friends understood the horror that had destroyed our families. And they could, thinking back on the many months of anxiety, flight, dissimulation, and close calls with disaster, fashion in their minds a narrative of their lives that was entirely convincing to them. There were good people and bad people in this narrative. Their wartime mental tableaux resembled those huge fourteenth-century Italian frescoes of the Last Judgment, painted during the disastrous pandemic known as the Black Death: a vast number of damned souls subjected to indescribable suffering often on the right side of the Ultimate Judge and those happy few who had been saved on his other. For Salonica's Jews who had survived (but obviously not only for them) their images of the very recent past were filled by innumerable innocent lives lost, as well by criminals, mostly Germans and locals, but also some Jews. There was also a beginning and an end to their stories, which began, if not in March 1943, perhaps a couple of years earlier, with the Germans' arrival in their city. No sooner had they made their way back home, nearly all of them experienced a sudden, apocalyptic epiphany of the tragedy that had been consummated in the preceding several months. They knew that they were now condemned to live, as survivors, in a world that had been turned upside down. The city of their dreams had become a city of ghosts.

As for me, blissfully unaware as I was of what was going on, daily life continued to unfold, slowly and routinely, in our little house in Vizyinou Street. Thinking back onto this stretch of time, I am aware that what has stuck in my mind are a few sparse episodes, moments plucked out of a much larger tableau: events, or happenings that left an imprint I have carried with me for the past many years. I mentioned a few in the preceding chapter. I shall describe a few more below. The point is that it is difficult for me now to remember, much less to find the words with which to describe, the texture and the cadences of my everyday life. Given the lack of these memories, it is even more difficult to explain why, as long as two or three years following our return to Evzonon Street, I would scribble down letters to *Yiayià* Harikleia, expressing my yearning to see her again and closing my letters with a deeply felt "with all my love." I wish I could somehow get my hands on these letters. But I do remember all too well the little drawings that decorated the margins of my messages to my "grandmother" in Athens, and my excitement when listening to my father or mother read out to me the responses that would arrive from Athens.

I do not think I felt any great privations during that period. On the contrary, in my naiveté, or was it my innocence, largely undisturbed, I trundled along enjoying whatever distractions were within easy reach. Of course, in retrospect, I realize that my diet, like every other person's diet in wartime Greece, was poor; food was neither abundant nor especially appetizing. But, for lack of anything better, I did not seem to mind. Nor did I seem to mind my return to a mostly solitary life, having now been removed from the daily companionship I enjoyed in the Kalkou household. No whining, no nightmares, no outbursts of unhappiness marked my days. Under the surface, there was tension that was beginning to brew, but it did not come up to the surface for a while. Perhaps my muted reaction, at least in the first weeks of my cohabitation with my mother, was itself an unrecognized realization of the circumstances in which we lived. I doubt it. Or was I limited by my lack of imagination, by my persistent failure to grasp the alternatives that faced me and my folks in those sad and curious days?

I already described the day-long motorcycle adventure through the mountains near Athens in my mother's futile search for traces my father may have left during his nearly year-and-a-half-long absence. This was in mid- or late October 1944. It had to be after 14 October when, as I recently discovered by consulting historical accounts of the period, the first British troops arrived in Athens. I remember very well my mother's return home late that day. Emotionally, she was in tatters. Her crying, and her intense description of the day's adventure to our two landladies shocked me. I had never seen my mother cry. For all the period since our move to Vizyinou Street, around me she had kept a serious but cool demeanor. To be sure, she was demanding in her expectations of me. I had to behave in a certain manner, which she approved of: no shouting, never forgetting to say please and thank you, being polite, sitting down at table for meals, thanking the Good Lord at the end of a meal, and, perhaps significantly, reciting a prayer before going to bed at night. In short, I had to conform my behavior to the canons of middle-class traditions, as my mother remembered them from her life in Salonica. In all this, she was a disciplinarian. A little later, her insistence on unquestioned discipline led to a major fiasco, when a few months later I tried to run away from home. I'll get to my revolutionary outbreak shortly. In the meantime, I should make it clear that her penchant for discipline was not related, directly at least, with her temper. As far as I remember, her nerves were never on show, at least until our return to Salonica. There, within a few weeks, she suffered a major breakdown. For many months her cries and shouts, while she was in bed at home, reverberated in my mind, creating an image of my mother that was in sharp contrast with the one I had formed in Athens. More than once since then, I wondered if the two sides of her personality—her wartime granite discipline and her emotional explosion after our return—were not two sides of the same coin, the latter being a response, or compensation of sorts, for the former.

My father returned to our house less than a month after my mother's day-long excursion. As I already wrote above, he found his way to our home in the middle of a mild late October night, shortly after the liberation of Athens from the Germans and the arrival of the Brits, but before the outbreak of fighting between rival groups of Greeks who had fought in the Resistance. He first went to the convent, there they pointed him in the direction of Mrs. Kalkou's house, and, finally, he made it to our house. I overcame the shock of his return quickly. The initial surprise of that seedy-looking, unknown intruder's presence in our room soon gave place to several hours of anxious curiosity. I was awakened in the midst of all the confusion and the agitated conversations between my parents and our two hostesses, who kept bursting into our room to check up on things. The long and loud process of cleaning him up, preparing the water and the sponges in the kitchen, fetching the steaming hot water in buckets to the bathroom, my mother's shrieks at the sight of lice, the awkward scissor jabs to snip his untended hair, and his protests to leave his hair alone—all this commotion startled and puzzled me. Then, after this ritual was completed, I kept thinking it was strange for this newcomer to be stretched out in my mother's bed. The timbre of his voice very much reminded me of Mr. Michalis (Bonomo was his name in Salonica), one of the two friends who had accompanied my parents in their escape from Salonica whom I had seen once or twice in Athens when he had accompanied Uncle Isaac in one of his visits to Vizyinou Street. His voice was easily recognizable, and, instinctively, I associated my father's voice with his.

Not least, my parents' language that night confounded me. I had no trouble following my father's conversation with the two other ladies of the house. "Difficult," it was difficult he kept repeating, but we made it. I was puzzled. What was it that was so difficult, and what was he able to achieve? In any case, who were the friends with whom he faced those difficult challenges? I could not understand the substance of the conversation, but his language was clear. He spoke in Greek, exclusively my everyday language for more than a year and a half. But when they spoke to each other, my parents used a language that was incomprehensible to me, even if the words I kept hearing may have reverberated in my mind as sounds I had once been familiar with. They reverted to their languages, the words and expressions that rooted them in their old, familiar homes: Ladino and French. They had not uttered a word in either language for the past year and a half. The freedom to speak as they wished, in whatever language they preferred, must have seemed like an omen of better times, a sign that life was returning to normal.

Throughout the night, lying in my bed, which was set at the foot of my mother's bed, I kept sliding under my sheets and blankets, covering my head as if I wanted to protect myself from an unknown peril. I do not know what they discussed that night. But I can guess: they had remained alive and free, even in the face of great danger; they had been lucky; they were beneficiaries of generous assistance from some people, even if they were surrounded by many more who seemed driven by a demonic determination to harm them. Their son had also made it, without any apparent damage to his body and his personality. To be sure, they talked about much more. They must have wondered about their families and friends in Salonica. There was no hint yet of their fate. My parents knew that family members, like all other Jews from Salonica, had been transported to Poland where the Germans had promised to settle them in new towns and furnish them with homes. Still, there had not been any news from them, following my blurting out when I first arrived in Athens, that grandpa and grandma had been taken. Taken where, by whom, by what means, were they now settled, was my grandfather faring well in his new home? His health had been cause for such concern in Salonica. And Marcelle, my mother's sister who had married in 1942 and was pregnant when the family was rounded up, how was she doing? And her husband, Pepo Carasso? All these questions remained unanswered and were cause of persistent confusion, if not yet panic. Did the postal service between Poland and Greece not work during wartime? Later, once in Salonica they mentioned this last question, only to remind themselves how almost willfully blind in their ignorance and naivety they had been.

About six months earlier, on Easter Sunday, I had not recognized my mother when she had approached me as I was standing next to the priest in the church yard. Now, in October, I faced a similar conundrum. For whatever reason—the abruptness and surprise of my father's arrival in the middle of the night, the many months since we had last been together, the absence of almost any reference to him during the previous year and a half—had ended up blurring any clear memory of his presence in my life. A shadow of his existence probably continued to lurk in my conscience, under the surface. But it was impossible for me to give a name to that shadow, to translate its outline into the image of a recognizable person. Although I have retained a vivid image of the scene in my mother's and my room in the hours after my father's arrival that evening, the fact is that I did not discern who the stranger was who popped up in my life unexpectedly. Since then, in the decades that followed, I often wondered about my failure to recognize either one of my parents, more or less one year after having been separated from them. Or, perhaps, I could not help but wonder if my amnesia had been in part voluntary, if I desired, deep down, to shield myself from my previous life, from which, step after step, I had been removed time and again.

The next morning, my mother left for work later than usual. Everyone in the house was smiling that day. *Yiayià* Harikleia had prepared a breakfast for my father that must have seemed extravagant to him. I remember the eggs she put on the table. What was the point of eating eggs in the morning, I wondered? The only eggs I remembered eating were those (never more than one at a time) served to me, invariably in the afternoon, by Soeur Anastasie at the convent. And all that touching of hands, my father's occasional caressing of her face as if he wanted to ensure that she was real, sitting there next to him, the evident pleasure each of them expressed at the other's presence, this was all new to me. It was also awkward and embarrassing. Such gestures of affection were unknown to me. They were alien to the habits I had passively acquired in the recent past. Over breakfast, my mother gave my father some money and a list of what to buy at the grocery store nearby. Her firm instructions to me were that I should lead my father to the grocery store, that I should not annoy him, and that, in general terms, I should do my best to be a good boy.

Later that morning, accompanied by Victor, always happy to be invited to come along, my father and I left. I held his hand and slowly led him toward the grocery story, the dog running before us, leading the way. I remember my feeling of pride and responsibility at being charged with leading an older man, whom in that very morning I had been strongly urged to call *babà*, even though I would need some time to sort out my ties to him. As I am struggling with these lines, I am once again befuddled by the distortions of time in my conscience, as the elision of those years drives images of a long time ago simultaneously back and forth from a distant past to a fleeting present and then back to the past. Here I am, close to my eighty-third birthday, trying to capture in my mind and define in words the reactions of a young boy I once knew well to a man who was about half the age I am today, but who, to that young boy, had the appearance of a mysterious older man. Once again, I am struggling with the words that convey something I sense but am not quite able to describe with precision. Perhaps the pleasure and the awkwardness of the situation I faced as I was walking with my father to purchase our provisions had a different source. Since my arrival in Athens, almost a year and a half earlier, I had not had any contacts with men: my universe comprised Soeur Hélène and the nuns at the convent, Mrs. Kalkou and her children, our two landladies in Vizyinou Street, and, of course, my mother. To be sure, there were my two uncles, but their occasional appearances were so brief I do not think my family ties to them had registered in my mind. Now, here I was, holding the hand of an older man, leading him on our way to run our errands. It was at once a strange and a pleasant experience. On the way, we passed the parrot's residence, for the encounter that flustered me to no end. The blasted bird refused to show off by singing his anti-Mussolini song. After the war, time and again my father drew on his ability to defuse thorny situations, especially when as president of a government-sponsored organization charged with administering properties of Jews who never returned from the camps, he often reconciled claimants who fought hard for properties they were convinced were theirs. That morning I witnessed for the first time his ability as conciliator, as he invented a perfect answer to pacify a little boy's sense of hurt caused by a dumb parrot's stubbornness.

At long last, after many months of separation, the family was once again united. In the preceding many months, each of us had been bounced about along complicated and constantly shifting itineraries. Our lives had lacked stability, but in one way or another each one of us had found his way to the meeting point in Vizyinou Street. My mother's persistence and courage were principally responsible for this success. But my father had also contributed mightily by surviving in conditions that were extremely difficult and challenging for someone his age and background. As for me, I had followed along, a dog's tail as it were, but always pliant, and chameleonic, able to adjust to new and unpredictable circumstances, a habit that I think has stood me well over the years. We should all have been happy, and, to a certain extent, we were. My parents were finally together. To an outsider, intimations of family bliss were discernible. At a practical level, things were not bad. My mother's position in the Red Cross provided sufficient income to make it possible for us to make ends meet and pay the rent of our convenient lodgings. I had found both parents, and slowly I was beginning to become reacquainted and feel comfortable with my father. His presence also helped me by placing his milder and more conciliatory personality as a buffer between myself and my mother's exigent expectations of me. *Atiò Lilica, laisse-le. Il est encore petit.* I first heard this refrain in his softly reproachful voice shortly after our reunion; it would become familiar to me in the years immediately after our return to Salonica, always expressed in that mixture of Ladino and French to which I would soon become accustomed.

As for my father, the first few weeks following his return, he spent much of his time building up his resilience, recovering not only from the previous months' physical and emotional strains, but also picking up his strength following a bout of typhus he had suffered in the mountains. On occasion, he would leave the house to reacquaint himself with Athens, sauntering about in parts of the city he liked best: Athinàs and Aiòlou streets and all the surrounding winding alleys, full as they were with small retail shops and artisan laboratories. After the war, once he started taking me with him on his periodic trips to Athens, he always found modest hotels in this area where we could stay, and more than once told me that this was the part of Athens he liked best. When once I asked him why, his simple answer was that it reminded him of the center of Salonica—Salonican Sephardic cosmopolitanism at its finest! On more than one occasion in his meanderings through the center of Athens, he tracked down his two brothers (Uncles Isaac and Raphael) who had themselves survived the war by hiding in various locations in Athens and were still waiting for an occasion to return to Salonica. His days were seemingly relaxed and aimless. Of course, he spent many hours with me, trying in his shy and awkward manner to draw me out and tease out of me descriptions of my recent experiences. Often, I fear that I let him down. As gentle and inviting as he tried to be, I sensed in him something formal, a distance he instinctively kept from others, even from me. I do not remember him being impatient or irritable. I even recall my mother telling me that he enjoyed my company and liked my behavior.

Even so, all along following his return, a penumbra of uneasiness and restlessness seeped into his behavior. He had had no news of his mother, and that silence greatly concerned him. He also worried a great deal about his business. Soon after arriving in Athens, Uncle Isaac passed on to him a letter (which is now in my possession) that had reached him early in July 1944. Dated 22 June of that year, the letter was written and signed by a presumed family friend, Mr. N. T., to whom in late 1942 and early 1943 my father had entrusted much of his store merchandise. The hope was that he would safeguard these goods and return them if someday we managed to get back. But now, in the summer of 1944, Mr. N. wrote that, unfortunately, following no fewer than three burglaries of his warehouse, all of my father's goods had disappeared. There was nothing left for him to return! My father never believed N.'s claims, especially in light of his sudden and unexplained enrichment after the war. A question haunted him: How would he start again? The Germans had ransacked his store, and the merchandise he thought was in safe hands had disappeared. There was also his anxiety about our situation in Salonica. What had happened to our house? And what about my grandmother's apartment? News from Salonica arrived in bits and pieces, the general picture there was fuzzy at best, and the concern about what was in store increased each passing day.

By mid-November, my father decided that he could no longer simply pass the time in Athens, waiting for someone to signal that he could leave. Come what may, he had to return to Salonica as soon as possible, and see for himself the remnants of our previous lives. His determination to leave was strengthened by the country's political conditions. With every passing day it was becoming clearer that, following the retreat of the Germans, an armed confrontation between the left and the right was likely to erupt. His time in the mountains had shown him the hostility—indeed, the visceral enmity—between different groups of the Resistance. The left-leaning guerrilla armies that had successfully fought the Germans believed that they enjoyed Stalin and Tito's encouragement to take over the country's government, while those on the right, urged by the king and his entourage and actively supported by Winston Churchill who a little later (25 December) visited Athens, were determined to restore the prewar balance between political forces and social classes. Once again, the air smelled of war, but this time it would be a war among brothers, the worst and bitterest kind of war. So, he decided to leave as soon as transport could be secured.

For anyone who remembers conditions in Greece during the years of the civil war, it is hard to imagine that through November 1944, it was still possible to travel between Athens and Salonica by land. If I am not mistaken, my father took a slow, commercial train, sometime late in November. Soon thereafter, with the outbreak of hostilities, it became impossible to travel by train or bus. My father disappeared from the house one evening after I had gone to sleep. I did not hear him leave nor do I remember my mother saying much about his departure. It was natural that she be of two minds about his plans. On the one hand, she obviously felt safer in his presence. On the other, she understood the need for him to precede our arrival in Salonica and secure housing and other necessities for us. I assume she reluctantly consented to his plan to leave. He left, so the explanation went, to see how grandpapa and grandmama were. We would soon join him. Later, I was told that *Yiayià* Harikleia tried to dissuade him claiming, not unreasonably, that it was still dangerous to leave. But he stuck to his decision. I do not recall my making a big fuss about his departure. After all, he had been with us only for about one month after an absence of more than a year. It seemed more natural for him to be away than to be present.

For my mother and me, the next five months, until mid-April 1945, were intensely agitated and full of adventure, perhaps the most dangerous since our move to Vizyinou Street. There were moments when even I became conscious of the danger, unlike my oblivious reactions to our previous circumstances and the close calls that I had lived through. Although there had been some desultory fighting in November, civil war in Athens erupted for real early in December in what are still remembered as the "December events." Soon fighting spilled out into the city's streets and squares. Both sides treated their opponents with unrestrained and triumphalist violence that rivaled German and Italian retaliations against the Resistance. The partisans would often occupy parts of town at night, only to retreat during the day when royalists, soon aided by British forces, would assert their presence. Curfews were tacitly respected, if for no other reason than to protect simple citizens from the risk of getting trapped in the crossfire of competing forces. Until the outbreak of urban hostilities, my mother had not felt insecure about my staying largely alone during the day, while she was at work in the center of town. But now she began to worry about leaving me at home. What might happen if she were blocked away from the house, unable to return for a day or more? Starting in mid-December, she got into the habit of often taking me with her to work, as she had on occasion done before. The close call in the tram shortly after she started working at the Red Cross was a reminder of the risks lurking in the streets of Athens. Only now the danger of getting sent to Auschwitz following a German dragnet had been replaced by the all too real possibility of being hurt in the crossfire or getting trapped away from home.

The mornings were fairly safe. We usually left home after breakfast and got with little difficulty to the Red Cross offices at the Marasleio School, not far from where, today, stand two of the most imposing postwar buildings in Athens, the Concert Hall and the American Embassy. The trouble was getting back, when, after the curfew, guns began to shoot and people had to duck behind improvised protective shields to avoid stray bullets. There was always an urgency about leaving work and making our way to Vizyinou Street. Frequently, by the time we hurriedly opened the side door into the garden, we could hear the sound of shooting, followed by the deep and ominous silences between gun shots. One day, I do not remember why, we left the office a tad late. She had delayed our departure for no more than half an hour, perhaps a good deal less. Yet, it was time enough to get in real trouble—or almost. As we were rushing down the streets to arrive at the tram stop with the sounds of gunshots reverberating against the house walls, we turned a corner and my mother stopped frozen in her tracks. A dead body was lying in the middle of the street. We never discovered where the mortal shot had come from nor who the poor devil was who had paid with his life for who knows what unforgivable sin. My mother held me tightly, pushed me against a house wall, and stood in front of me, offering her body as a shield. I do not know how long we stayed flattened and breathless against that wall, perhaps a few seconds only, probably a few minutes. But at a certain point, the door of a garden opened in front of us on the opposite side of the street, a man ran out, grabbed me, and lifted me onto his shoulder. He pushed my mother in the direction of the open door and shoved us both inside. We were dazed, my mother perhaps more than me. It was difficult to take in the surroundings. A lady came out into the garden with a glass of water for my mother and something (I wish I remembered what) for me to drink. The man said that, out of curiosity, he had peeked from behind the curtains to see what was going on in the street and spotted us defenseless in the middle of the shooting. Without a moment's hesitation, he dashed out in the garden, opened the door, and brought us into safety. All this I remember quite well. What I did not remember myself was the aftermath, recounted to me more than once later. It turns out that, after catching her breath, my mother, not wishing to be a nuisance to those nice people, ventured the thought that we should leave and try to get home. Nothing doing. Our hosts would have none of it. We would spend the night in their house; we could sleep in the living room. They would feed us, and the next morning, if things were quiet, we could leave. But if we wanted, we could stay longer.

Another close call! A few years later (perhaps in the spring of 1949 or 1950) when we had all three traveled to Athens so my father could tend to some of his affairs and my mother and I enjoy a brief holiday, my mother thought we should return to the scene of that adventure. She wanted to see that couple again, and thank them, however belatedly, for their generosity, indeed for their courage. She remembered neither their names nor the exact address of that accidental encounter. So, we set out one morning from our hotel near Omonia Square and walked around for a couple of hours. My mother was sure the house we were looking for was just around this corner, and then that one. But every time we came up blank. My father teased her once or twice, I whined along the way for all that aimless trapsing, and we gave up. We changed directions, and instead pointed to the Royal Garden. Ducks and swans, not to speak of the garden's magnificent vegetation offered a suitable mental escape from the memory of the shooting and the corpse.

Many times since, my mind floated back to that scene and to our rescue. It was such an intense experience, difficult to forget. In these moments of recollection, I could not escape the obvious thought that the spontaneous and selfless help offered by an anonymous man and his wife may have saved our lives. All three of us that morning, my father included, had wanted to find our rescuers and thank them. My father had quipped once or twice that it would be nice to see if, after all these years, they would recognize me. After all, now I wore long pants! Had we succeeded in our mission, they also might have been pleased, or so I suspect, perhaps a bit embarrassed but pleased nonetheless. But we did not succeed, and, naturally, we were disappointed. Yet, the point of it all was not that we thank them. The point was that selfless and courageous deeds such as theirs do not aim necessarily to garner someone's thanks and gratitude. Their action underscored the fact that decent people act in such

COURAGE AND COMPASSION

a way: just as the English soldier who had helped my mother in her trek through the mountains to locate my father and the anonymous man in the tram a few months before. Perhaps even the German soldier who had procured much needed medicines for my grandfather while we were still in Salonica? Is this last question a sacrilegious long shot?

You don't have to fight wars and win battles to be heroic. You can be a hero by performing small deeds away from public attention and the cheers of the crowds. This was my father's reflection that he patiently laid out to me in the train on our return to Salonica. To a small boy (I was then nine or ten) who had become a passionate fan of Achilles, it was a lesson that stuck, for all my doubts during that long train ride.

My mother and I continued living in Vizyinou Street following my father's departure. But, for the first time since our reunion following my move from Mrs. Kalkou's home, a certain amount of irritation was evident in her behavior, and the beginning of a modest degree of rebelliousness began coloring my responses to her. Initially, nothing dramatic happened. Possibly, my father's absence put my mother's nerves more on edge than before. Perhaps the daily uncertainty and danger to and from work, as, from the end of November, acts of violence were increasingly punctuating the city's daily life; perhaps also news from Salonica was intimating to her that the road into the future was even more uncertain, while the return to the beginning we had left behind would be more arduous than she had imagined. It is also possible that with the slow passage of time I grew increasingly tired and impatient with my days of sloth and boredom at the Red Cross. Every time I return in my mind to that situation, I am struck by how my daily existence those days was different from my life in the preceding many months.

Now, with my mother almost constantly at my side, my life was closely regulated, even in those stretches of time when she was at work, and I at home under the distant but not terribly vigilant observation of our two landladies. In the convent and with Mrs. Kalkou, I was even freer. As long as I did not get myself in trouble, I could do what I wanted. There was no pressure to do this or that, to follow a strict routine. If I can extrapolate from two or three years later, my mother's serious and repeated urging to me was that I had become a big boy and must behave like one, especially when my father was occupied with his business. No need to be told again and again what to do and how. It was enough to be conscious of my role and discharge it. I suspect that this message had begun to seep in my consciousness, and, initially unawares but increasingly more sharply, it had begun to gnaw at me.

I have tried many times to remember the spark that triggered the rebellion. Even when we were in the United States, I asked my mother if she remembered. She always claimed she did not. Was it something she said or did? Or perhaps a sudden spark of disobedience that lit the fire and provoked the drama? Of the many events, and places and people I have forgotten from that stretch of time, this is probably the one that I regret most deeply not remembering with greater precision.

The fact is that sometime in late December or January (1945), in the middle of a day when my mother was home, I decided that I simply could no longer tolerate my living conditions. I had to leave home. That day, unusually, there had been much commotion and shouting at Papadiamanti Square, a block and a half from home. All the noise tickled my imagination and led me to action. So, quietly I went into our room while my mother was occupied with other things, pulled out of a closet a small sheet, laid it out onto the bed, and selected some clothes that seemed necessary for the new life, far from my mother and other supervisors, I was about to begin: some underwear and socks, a sweater, one or two shirts, one pair of short pants (the only kind I had), and a pair of shoes. I remember the shoes, because I hesitated taking them; they were so heavy! I wrapped everything in that sheet, tied it so that nothing would fall out, and, tiptoeing, I carefully opened the garden door onto the street. I was escaping! I had no idea where I wanted to go. But I went, as I would go many other times in the future, unsure of my destination. Shortly before writing this paragraph, I accidentally came across something written by T. S. Eliot in 1931. In a letter, the great poet mused that "it comes as a surprise to me and always as a kind of shock when I realise for a moment the continuity in most people's lives. Whereas for me . . . life has been discontinuous." Is it nearly blasphemous to invoke the great man's thought when referring, however much in passing, to a small boy's folly? Yet, T. S. Eliot's words lend shape to a thought that has been central to me, while also giving meaning to my act of rebellion in January 1945. Discontinuity was at once my goal and my strategy, even at the tender age of not quite six.

I stepped out onto the street, turned right at our door, walked the half block where I turned left onto the street that led to the noise and the crowds, and proceeded toward the square. The distance between the corner where I turned left, and my provisional destination must not be more than a few hundred meters. It takes no more than six to seven minutes to walk. Yet, it was enough for my mother's *longa manus* to go into action. It turns out that she realized what I was up to and very discreetly began following me down the street. At the corner where I turned left, she saw a policeman, to whom she explained what was going on. Before I knew it, a tall man in uniform was standing next to me. He took my hand and in a soft voice asked me what I was doing. I explained that I had left home and had no desire to go back. Shall we continue together? he asked. I had no objection, and readily gave him my hand.

Slowly, we reached the square, where a larger crowd than I had ever seen were milling about. Hundreds, perhaps thousands of people were jammed there, shouting, talking to each other, some singing songs I did not know. The policeman continued holding my hand, as we slowly snaked our way through the crowd. All of a sudden I froze, stunned by the spectacle before me. At the other end of the square from where we had arrived, a platform had been constructed, surrounded by a small band of armed men. I looked up, craning my neck to see the platform, and there, less than a stone's throw from where I was standing, was a spectacle I have remembered all my life: four men were hanging there, heads drooping onto their necks, their bodies inert slowly moving back and forth in the breeze. My head began to swirl and frightened beyond words impulsively I started pleading with the policeman to take me back to my mother. My guard slowly turned around, and I with him.

There behind us was my mother! It was a miracle, something magical my child's mind could not grasp. How could she know where I was? How did she guess that I so badly wanted to be with her? I lunged at her and grabbed her. The policeman looked at my mother, assuming no doubt, that she would agree with what he intended to tell me. Then, he turned his gaze toward me, and sternly told me one of the meanest things anyone has ever told me: You see what happens to little boys who run away from home! In that place and time, it was probably the sort of advice one could expect from a guardian of the public order. If his intention had been that I not forget that episode, he was entirely successful. That moment has remained almost as alive in my mind as it was then. But for me, the lesson was not entirely what that policeman intended to dispense to a foolish little boy. To be sure, it was a lesson about leaving home—a lesson that I repeatedly violated in the years to come. Perhaps more importantly, it was a lesson about war, especially about the brutality of civil war. The dead body my mother and I had witnessed lying in the middle of a street a few weeks earlier had not made such an impression on me, probably because of the lightning speed sequence of our being pulled over to safety. There was no time to absorb the spectacle of that body. But now, here were four dead men, staring at me, as it were. Their contorted bodies were witnesses of the violence they had suffered before their deaths.

That scene was incomprehensible to me. To an adult present in Papadiamanti Square that day, and to me every time I have since lingered over that frightful image, there was nothing incomprehensible: four partisans of the left had been hunted down and murdered by their enemies on the right. I have no doubt that, some other time and in another place, the roles of left and right in such a brutal ritual would be reversed, and that violence—blind violence—would prevail, as it almost always does in any war between brothers.

8.
A City of Ghosts

Sometime in the 1990s, a young English anthropologist decided to devote her doctoral dissertation to the survivors of the Shoah in Salonica. She traveled to the city and spent some time collecting oral testimonies of a small number of elderly Jews who were still living there. Her informants had either survived the German occupation hidden in Greece or had lived through the horrors of the concentration camps and managed to make their way back to the city of their birth. One of the witnesses who spoke with her, it seems extensively, was an elderly lady variously identified as M, or L, or LM. This loquacious lady said that, after about two years spent hiding mostly in Athens, she had herself returned to Salonica in April of 1945. Together with other survivors, she waited anxiously for the return of her family and friends. It was only about a month later, starting in May, that far-fetched news of what had happened in the camps began to trickle back to the city and to be heard for the first time by the incredulous survivors.

Her interlocutor told the young anthropologist that when the truth about her family began to sink in—they had all been murdered in Auschwitz—she "went crazy." From that point on, she reminisced that for her "the city . . . was like a ghost." Whenever she walked the streets, or visited once familiar sites, or even lingered in her very own house, she was overwhelmed by the sense that people she knew should have been there. But they were not. All these relatives, neighbors, friends, classmates, and teachers had disappeared. Her world had been wiped out; its inhabitants murdered in faraway places. How could she come to terms with this cruel absence? Could she continue living in Salonica, when her every breath and every move was a reminder that her world had been violently, barbarously destroyed? And how could she confront her profound and corrosive sense of guilt that she had survived while the people dearest to her had not? Might her very survival have contributed to the deaths of her parents and siblings? Could she have done something more than she did to save them? Almost immediately after her return and her discovery that now her city was a ghost—or, as distinguished Anglo-American historian Mark Mazower wrote in his very fortunate history of the city a few years after that oral interview, that Salonica had now become "a city of ghosts"—she decided to get out. She had to leave.

A few years later, accompanied by her family she moved to the United States, where she lived for about forty years. There, she found pleasure in her success, although peace of mind continued to elude her. She began her university studies, which she had never had a chance even to begin in Salonica, ended up obtaining a Ph.D. and was appointed to a series of mostly satisfying professional positions. Her neighbors and colleagues treated her with respect, recognizing not only her professional success, but acknowledging the difficult circumstances of her life, before and after her arrival to North America. Then, having been left a widow, and with her children settled on their own, she returned once again to Salonica, where her brothers-in-law's families and some friends of old had over the years repeatedly beckoned her to come back. Their letters since her departure had been reminders that the cozy sociability of a small group of French- and Ladino-speaking Sephardic Jews would welcome her and provide her with friendship and psychological support. She had much to share with them. They, also, had lived through experiences similar to her own. Their memories of wartime and of prewar Salonica offered a common bond that was altogether different from the sincere if not always emotionally satisfying professional acquaintances she had acquired in the United States. It is true that in Salonica she missed the intensity and excitement of the professional routine she had discovered in the United States, and the very rich cultural, especially musical, life that had become an integral part of her existence in Cleveland, Ohio. Yet, Salonica offered its own compensations. Besides the old friendships that were now renewed in her and her friends' slowly setting old age, in Salonica living conditions were easier than they had been in the United States. The pleasant Mediterranean climate, not to mention the easy proximity to the sea that she so dearly loved, the tastes and smells that reminded her of her youth helped her adjust to her old hometown, even though the Salonica of old was gone forever. However, it would be an exaggeration to suggest that the passage of time, her return to the city of her birth, and the slow softening of emotions had reconciled her to her turbulent life during the Shoah. She was not unhappy about having returned. But the ghosts of old had not altogether abandoned her. Ghosts have a way of hanging around and continuing to haunt their victims. There may have been a darker side in her decision to return, a side she did not often discuss with others, but which was probably born of her feelings of guilt toward her husband. His intensely unhappy transition to his new American life stood in sharp contrast to her very satisfying series of successes. But I am now getting ahead of myself. Let me linger a bit more over the ghosts and the city they colonized immediately after the war.

A city of ghosts—this lady's metaphor about Salonica is striking. She was not the only war survivor to draw on this metaphor when confronting the spectacle of peace at war's end. The stench of death and the nearly palpable survival of the dead in the imagination of the living seem to have led, almost naturally, to this metaphor. No lesser a poet than T. S. Eliot in his visit to Paris in 1945 wrote to a friend that the city had become a city of ghosts.

The elderly lady who, about half a century after the war, spoke with such emotional pungency about the persistent presence of ghosts in her life was Lily Molho, my mother. If I am not mistaken, that interview was one of her first articulated attempts to work through the maze of her postwar memories. It took years for her to muster the strength to speak with such candor to a stranger about these matters. But even in the 1990s, back to the *douceur de vie* of her provincial birthplace, she could hardly bring herself to face up to a question that, on occasion, some of her friends ventured to ask her. How could she reconcile her immediate postwar intense dislike of *los griegos* and her return to Greece in her advanced old age? Cleveland had offered much psychological sustenance for her. Its institutions had opened unimagined professional possibilities to an immigrant who had only her own resources to draw on, unsupported as she was by networks of friends and relatives.

The Salonica she evoked in her conversations in the 1990s was the city to which she and I had returned in the spring of 1945. For those who had known it before 1943, this was a different city, having now been shorn of its defining characteristic of the prewar period, a trait repeatedly described by members of the allied expeditionary force that had been stationed in the city's outskirts during World War I. Thirty years later, no one could venture to describe it as the New Jerusalem or the Jerusalem in the Balkans. Its Jews were now gone, or largely gone; Salonica had become the Greek state's co-capital. An intense nationalist ideology had replaced its multicultural and multiethnic coloration. The old Salonica had disappeared, definitively, it seemed, absorbed by the now hegemonic Hellenic and Christian Orthodox monolingual ideology and its intensely cultivated suspicion of outsiders.

It took time—more than a handful of years—for me to decipher my mother's perception of Salonica and to understand the emotional burden she carried for decades after the war. Things were different, at once a little more complicated, and a little simpler, in the months she and I continued to live in Athens. My father had left for Salonica in late November 1944. We made it back in April 1945. This was the stretch of time—about five months—when she prepared me for what lay ahead.

Only her predictions were wildly off the mark, so deeply were they colored by her nostalgia for her previous life. In those months, she wistfully cultivated ideas about family life as she remembered it, telling me stories about her parents, her brother and his faithful white poodle, her sister Marcella and Marcella's baby, my cousin, who was certainly born by then, and about my father's business, which, she naturally assumed, I would one day inherit. Her existence in the previous two years had been a series of adventures and interruptions. One surprise after another had shaken her life, pointing it in new and unimagined directions: a hard-to-believe escape through the mountains; a stretch of time as a family cook, then as a maid, then after that, a clerk; a series of extremely dangerous brushes with German-imposed law; nearly inconceivable decisions to entrust her son to people and institutions she knew nothing about; her separation from her husband who had simply disappeared for a long time. She had assumed all these new roles under a dissimulated identity, not only of her religion but of a past that she concealed under her new name. What was the point of all this suffering and uncertainty and of the repeated brushes with the law if not her own survival and that of her husband and son? For all three of us, she yearned, once these horrors would come to an end, to return to Salonica and pick up the threads of our life as it had been—or almost as it had been—before our escape in March 1943. In her imagination, continuity of affections, customs, and traditions would govern her life. Was it unreasonable for her to dream such dreams? Should she have understood that an incalculable disaster had forever changed the contours of her life? Given her family's history before the Shoah, it might be reasonable to give her the benefit of the doubt. After all, the lives of her parents and grandparents had all been rooted in one place, Salonica. Their ordered and comfortable homes had shielded her and her close relatives from major disasters. Wars, catastrophic fires, even financial crashes had not shaken their faith in the stability and viability of their way of life. She probably kept a reserve of skepticism about the images she conveyed to me during these months. But if she did, she certainly did not show it. As far as I remember, I was becoming increasingly upbeat about our return to Salonica. A whole new world waited for me there.

Only a few weeks after our return when the reality of the Shoah had sunk in did she realize how deep and permanent the caesura of the previous few years had been. It was no longer possible to think of life as a straight line, a continuous stream of more or less predictable events of a slowly unfolding routine. From then on, surprises, improvisation, readjustments, unexpected turns would become the order of the day. And this condition would continue after the family's decision to move to North America. Flux and adjustment would now set the cadences of her life. Strangely, or perhaps fatefully, she had been forced to return to the form of existence that had governed the histories of distant ancestors who, chased by enemies almost as dangerous as the Nazis were, had been expelled from Spain and Portugal and, traipsing across half of Europe, found their way to Salonica and other port cities of the Ottoman Empire.

Following the tragicomedy of my attempted getaway, we spent the winter planning our return home. Of course, I was no more than a passive observer in these preparations. I think they were coordinated by both my parents, although I do not know how they managed to communicate with each other. But they stayed in touch because I remember at least one piece of news my mother gave me, following a letter (or, more improbably, a telephone call) from my father: we would travel to Salonica by sea. Perhaps so as not to scare me, she did not explain why it was unwise to travel overland. Although Athens and other urban centers had by now been pacified, the civil war engulfed the countryside, interrupting rail and bus service between the country's north and south. I had not been near the sea for almost two years. Now, for me, the idea of it was a huge novelty, and my mother spent hours talking to me about it. She explained that for the first few years of my life, the sea had been a stone's throw from our house. Long walks in Salonica on the waterfront, visits to my grandmother's home on the corniche, excursions to inviting beaches at the city's edge had been frequent family activities. At least, these were my mother's recollections, and she talked to me about them time and again. These very early memories, and the pleasures my mother insisted on attaching to the sea had simply disappeared from my mind. With the arrival of spring (1945), the sea had become a recurrent theme in our conversations. It is perhaps the most intense memory I have of those weeks. It was also perhaps the reason for my eagerness to spend as much time as I could at the beach immediately after our return to Salonica and for my life-long love of swimming and simply spending hours sitting on the waterfront taking in the spectacle of the open sea with the endless satisfactions it offers to the senses.

The two very intense experiences following my father's departure for Salonica marked our daily routines in the following months. Our momentary but all too real encounter with the civil war in the streets of Athens, as we almost literally stumbled onto the body of a person who had been shot dead by an invisible executioner for no evident reason; and the equally real aftermath of the civil war, when I came face to face with the gruesome spectacle of the four dead men hanging in public view in Papadiamanti Square, casualties of an act of a revenge that was beyond my comprehension then and has remained largely incomprehensible since then. Years later, as these two cinematic scenes have regularly returned to my mind, it has seemed to me that their memory explains my wonder, almost my astonished recognition, at seeing for the first time in 1977 Goya's *Disasters of War* at the Prado. If nothing else, my two experiences had convinced my mother that extreme danger was ever present and that extra precautions were necessary to safeguard us both. Even if the Germans had been forced out of the country and the vile activities of their spies and collaborators been largely eliminated, other dangers, less predictable but no less worrisome, continued to threaten us. It was essential that I be shielded from every imaginable danger and carefully monitored at all hours of the day.

My principal memory of the months that followed those two events is that nothing much happened to me. Inactivity was the order of my days; boredom my state of mind. I was now carefully enclosed in the house and the garden; our two landladies became more punctilious overseeing my whereabouts, insisting that I snap to attention every time they asked me to show up; Uncle Isaac, hiding in his pockets pieces of chalk that I much treasured, appeared more frequently than before, while my mother took me with her to work only on special occasions. I remember well one or two them, as then I was given the food rations that were assigned to every Red Cross employee. A nice moment was a long walk through the center of Athens with my Uncle Roufa/Nicos who showed me some of the sights and, as he repeatedly did after the war, made me laugh at the unusual and funny stories he had such a knack at recounting. All the Molho adults present in Athens those days had been mobilized to provide protection and entertainment. My bonds with these two uncles were forged during the last months of our Athenian "exile," and they remained very strong for the rest of their lives, Isaac dying in the summer of 1983, Roufa in the autumn of 1997. If during these months I ever desired to see my friend the parrot I was invariably accompanied by an adult and never allowed to meander in the neighborhood on my own. During one of these visits, the parrot's owner emerged onto his porch and, trying to teach me the anti-Mussolini song, sang it with the colorful bird in what I enthusiastically thought was a nicely coordinated duet. My first concert! That song stuck with me, and for years thereafter, whether the occasion warranted it or not, I would hum or sing it to the amusement of any adult around me. Uncle Roufa/Nicos seemed to take especial pleasure hearing me sing it, probably because he had himself been conscripted and sent to the Albanian front at the time of Italy's invasion of Greece in 1940.

In retrospect, one of the benefits of those rather boring weeks, was my being introduced to the world of letters. Grandma Harikleia, wishing to divert my artistic energies which, after every one of Uncle Isaac's visits, produced large chalk smudges on every imaginable surface in the garden and the corridor leading to the house entrance, suggested that I use the chalk to learn how to write. She would offer me instruction every day, about half an hour or so, outside in the garden. There, ever so slowly, awkwardly holding a piece of chalk, I began to scribble individual letters of the Greek alphabet. I do not remember being especially interested in the exercise nor, certainly, was I especially good at it. Later, one of my undoubtedly self-serving justifications for my slow progress in learning how to read was that I had no books during those years. Reading became an infinitely pleasurable discovery only after our return to Salonica. But, in Vizyinou Street, after great difficulty with the letter omega, I managed to write my name, a feat that rather satisfied me, and gave my mother false hopes about my intellectual promise.

Outings in those months were infrequent. This is probably why I remember well the few visits to the Kalkou family where I would spend a day at a time in the children's company. I enjoyed playing with them, and I remember with great fondness their openness and willingness to let me participate in their activities. I liked especially Panayotis, the eldest of the five children, who, I suspect, was charged with keeping a careful eye on me. After the war, on a couple of occasions he came up to Salonica to spend a few weeks with us in a summer cottage we had rented in a seaside village (Epanomì) near Salonica. There, he helped me learn how to ride a bicycle, an ability that for years reminded me of his pleasant personality and helpful assistance.

As time went on, our preparation for the much-anticipated departure became more intense. My curiosity grew keener by the day, as my expectations had been piqued by my mother's stories. Who knows what I had been expecting. Nothing less than happiness, satisfaction, and endless carefree hours splashing in the beach waters near home! Of course, my father, whose presence was woven into most of my mother's stories about our future in Salonica, was another attraction in my imagination. Surely he would have spent time with me, entertaining me as he had done in our joint introduction to the parrot. The visit to Soeur Hélène and the other nuns at the convent was a sign that preparations were coming to a head. It was at once a ceremonial and a deeply felt personal occasion, a thank you and a farewell. I spent a short time with the nuns, especially with Soeur Anastasie, while my mother was in Soeur Hélène's study. Then I was called in myself. I vaguely remember my short meeting with the nun who had been instrumental in my salvation and that of my parents. Her appearance was at once severe but not unfriendly, and I did not feel out of place. I felt even more comfortable when, somewhat ritually, she gave me a small chocolate that she urged me to eat slowly so as to enjoy it to the fullest. After some pleasant banter, we took leave of her. Her last gesture took me by surprise. Having placed her hand on my head, she bent down, looked me in the eye and blessed me. She spoke in French, and I did not understand what she said. My mother thanked her once again, the two of them embraced, and we took our leave from the convent of Pammakaristos.

I am not sure why our departure was set for mid-April. No doubt the pleasant spring weather was a consideration, the fact that Easter was in the middle of the month, probably my father's urging that it was time for us to start on our way, and a suitable boat schedule that was most likely found by someone at the Red Cross. We left from the port of Lavrion, about 60 kilometers from Athens. I suspect that the port's condition in April 1945 bears little resemblance to its attractive image today. As I am trying to reconstruct whatever details of that trip linger on in my mind, I am struck, once again, by the absence of any memories, especially of one particular detail. How did we arrive at the port from Vizyinou Street? The distance is not small, perhaps more than 60 kilometers. Did we take a taxi, or did someone from the Red Cross or even from the convent take us there? I should remember this detail, because a ride in a private car would have been a big novelty for me. I do not think I had ridden in a car even once. Nor do I have any recollection of our adieus from our landladies whose pleasant hospitality had helped us spend several rather comfortable months in their home. I wonder, did I take my leave of the parrot, and of Victor, the neighbors' very friendly dog? Leave taking was always complicated during those two years, and each major move left almost no traces in my memory. The emotional weight must have been difficult to carry.

I do remember all too clearly our presence in the boat, although one not especially significant detail later became an issue of disagreement with my mother. She insisted that we had traveled in a cabin but left it only when the big storm we encountered made us both feel very uncomfortable. I remember nothing of a cabin but have a clear image in my mind of our being seated among a large crowd of other passengers in the common seating areas. It is not a big issue, but in this instance as well the different recollections point to the fragility of our memories of events that took place a long time ago. I had looked forward to my encounter with the sea, to seeing for myself the pleasures I had repeatedly heard recounted by my mother. Another surprise! Soon after leaving the port, we ran into a big storm, and I discovered, for the first time, the changing faces of the sea. The boat rocked violently, very soon everyone became sick to their stomachs, people were vomiting, some of them bending overboard, others shouting or praying. It was a mess. Until then my mother had never mentioned to me anything about storms. After that night, nobody had to describe to me what a sea storm was. In the midst of the mayhem, I learned the lesson well. The water's menacing dark colors, the wind whipping up huge, froth-covered waves, sailors unsteady on their feet, moving among the passengers trying to encourage them and assist those who seemed frozen in fear, all this left a big impression on me. I imagine that during the voyage, my mother did not feel or look much better than I did. As the boat was rocking, and water splashed in the sitting areas, I remember looking puzzlingly to her trying to understand how I should behave. I do not think I had ever felt so helpless. Someone must have taken pity on me, and, as I was holding for dear life on to a rail, out of the blue, a naked plastic doll was placed on my lap. Neither my mother nor I noticed who the very generous and charitable fellow passenger was who took pity on me. But I held tight on to the doll and was still holding it when, at dawn, I woke up from what must have been a deep sleep. For years after, I remembered the experience of the storm and my uncomfortable feeling in the few hours it took us to get through it. It had not been a pleasant experience nor one I would soon forget! In the summer before going to boarding school when I was twelve, I was taken by my mother to the cinema to see a movie about the Flying Dutchman. I understood nothing about the plot. But no sooner had we left the movie theater, than I told my mother that the film, with its dramatic storm, reminded me of our boat trip back to Salonica.

The trip took all night and a good part of the next day. By the time we entered the waters near Salonica, the weather had turned beautiful, the deep blue sea was calm, and the city's sights began appearing on the horizon. For years thereafter, perhaps to this very day, whenever I think of Salonica, I can't help but picture the scene that slowly took shape in the horizon that day as we slowly approached the port. Behind us, covered in snow (something I had never seen before) was Mount Olympus in all its majestic mystery, while facing us was the city, dominated, immediately behind it, by Mount Hortiatis covered in gray and mauve colors that would, over time, become a familiar sight to me. And right in front of us, ever closer to it as we approached the port was the White Tower, as much Salonica's symbol as the Acropolis is of Athens or the Statue of Liberty of New York. I sat staring at the spectacle, unable to decide if the scene that was unfolding before me was buried somewhere deep in my mind, an unacknowledged memory of a long-gone experience. The fact is that I more or less sat transfixed staring at the spectacle, unwilling to follow some other children who were running back and forth from one side of the boat to the other. Now I know, from photographs in my possession, that I had been in the White Tower park before we had left the city. But did I recognize the site on the day of my return to Salonica?

The closer we approached the quay, the greater the agitation in the boat. People were exclaiming at the sight, some were running in circles, others pointing to what I would later learn were the city's eastern suburbs where beaches and taverns were located, while a few others, for reasons I did not understand, were crying. One lady dressed in black, approached my mother, and tearfully explained that she was returning home, not knowing if anyone was waiting for her. My mother tried to console her. If she needed help, she said, my father and we would be glad to offer a hand. Then, in the middle of the confusion of disembarkation, the lady was lost in the crowd, and I never found out the reason for her unhappiness. I do not think she was Jewish. Just another victim of the war or of the civil war that was raging in the countryside.

The boat slowly reached the quay, near Aristotle Square, a short walk from Freedom Square, where three years earlier, my father had been badly beaten by the Germans. Only later did my mother explain the irony of that scene, but by then her descriptions were deeply colored by bitterness and anger. A small crowd of people—onlookers, friends, and relatives of passengers—was waiting on the quay. This time I had no trouble identifying my father. Alone, wearing a short-sleeved shirt, he had come to greet us, a huge smile on his face. Who knows what fears and hopes he harbored in his mind. After all, he had been in Salonica for almost five months and knew much more about what was awaiting us there. But the weather was beautiful, the joy of return was evident in my parents' faces, and I was happy. Things were fine. While my parents kissed each other, I kept tugging my father's arms, expecting I know not exactly what. We did not have much baggage, a couple of bags of clothing, my mother's purse with various documents, which someone shortly after our disembarkation wanted to inspect, and that mysterious doll onto which I was still clinging as if it had been mine for years. My father called one of the porters, who with their carts were waiting for passengers to summon them, and off we went. We walked along the waterfront, my parents pointed out my grandmother's apartment but told me that she would be staying with us and that, in fact, she was waiting for us at home.

Less than half an hour later, walking slowly as my parents were bombarding each other with questions and information, while I was doing my best to keep up with the porter's snappy pace, we turned left onto Evzonon Street, and a couple of blocks further to number 24. Did I enter instinctively into the garden entrance, or was I nudged by one of my parents? I had left the house on a dark night, on 21 March 1943, hidden in a blanket tightly held by my mother, lest someone recognize that a child was being carried from the city's Jewish quarters to a Christian home. I returned a little more than two years later, on 16 April 1945, a bright and sunny day, freely running toward our family home, no one seemingly caring where I was going or from where I had come. Once on the grounds of our house, I became aware of about a dozen people, silently staring at us, uncertain themselves of what the homeowners' reappearance implied for their own lives. No one greeted us, no one rushed to congratulate us on our return. My father ran up the one flight of stairs, vigorously opening our apartment door for us. Much more slowly, with a pained look deeply marking her face, my mother climbed the stairs of the home where she had spent her life from the time she was six years old, in 1921, until 1943, when she had left, pushed away by her all too realistic fears about the future. She entered the house hesitantly, and, sobbing, threw herself in her mother-in-law's open arms. My grandmother gathered the three of us around her and, in her strong voice, emotionally recited a Hebrew prayer thanking the Lord for our return. Within a few seconds, all three adults were sobbing, my grandmother, between sobs and smiles, hugging me repeatedly and saying things I did not understand. Then my parents, led by Grandmother Flora, began inspecting the house. I followed them for a few minutes, observing the rooms, and the sparse furniture left in them. As far as I remember, the house was not in terrible shape, even if my mother kept pointing to things that were not there, above all her piano. Strange that, after our return, the piano, and music making, which had occupied such a dominant place in my mother's life, fast receded into the background. Once a new piano was brought into the house a few weeks after our arrival, it sat in a corner of the sitting room, rarely touched by my mother. She just could not bring herself to make the music that had given her and her parents such pleasure. For all my father's pleading that she play the pieces by Schubert and Chopin that she had so loved, she steadfastly refused to do so. I recall her shaking her head and softly responding, in French, that it was not the right moment. Once or twice, in the winter after Marcella, my sister, was born, gathered as we were all around the woodstove in the sitting room, she finally opened the cover, sat before the keyboard, and produced a torrent of notes that left all of us spellbound. Then, after those handful of performances, nothing. Silence. Her piano playing belonged to another age, which like the old Salonica that vanished after that terrible spring of 1943, had itself disappeared into the mists of the past.

Once I stopped trailing the adults, the first thing I did was to venture hesitantly toward the back terrace overlooking our house's large garden. It was as if I were sleepwalking, instinctively driven toward places I subconsciously knew were there, but which I did not really remember. Was I discovering or rediscovering my home? As I opened the big French doors onto the terrace, the big garden was spectacularly stretched out before me. On the left, all along its length was a big wall, more than two meters high, separating our grounds from those of our Armenian neighbor's house. Covering the wall was a glorious wisteria in full bloom. I was dazed by its colors and its indescribable fragrance. For years thereafter, the image of that enormous, imposing wisteria remained fixed in my mind, an inseparable part of our house. Upon my first trip back to Salonica from the United States in the summer of 1962, one of my very first questions to the folks who were living in our house was about the wisteria. Was it still there, I wanted to know, did it continue to bloom every spring? It did. Someone fetched me a chair, and I sat under it, letting my mind drift, guided it seemed by the wisteria's colors and fragrance, to the moment of our return to our home and the years immediately following. When, a few years later, to my indescribable sadness, our house was sold and demolished by its new owner to make room for one of those grotesque apartment buildings that disfigured street after street in Salonica, the wall separating our house from that of our neighbors and the wisteria that adorned it were retained and survived for several years. Then, in 1982, when I took my new wife to show her the places of my youth, the wisteria was gone. But the whole neighborhood was gone—the house, the garden, the friends, their parents, the shoemaker whose store was on our building's ground floor, the pretty girl and her brothers who lived across the street in one of the small semi-basement apartments where refugees from Asia Minor were living—they were all gone.

At the moment of our return, on 16 April 1945, the wisteria reinforced my happy disposition, my happiness at our having returned. In contrast to the wisteria, the garden offered a desolate sight. The fruit trees had not been pruned in years, their mostly dried branches drooping from their trunks, the flower beds had all disappeared, their place taken by a large bomb shelter that someone had constructed during the war. For all the years following, the shelter's entrance—a big, ugly hole—repulsed me. I think only once did I venture in with a couple of friends to explore its dark and humid interior. At the garden's end, the gardener's small house was still in place, a policeman and his wife standing guard in front of it, seemingly protecting their new home from the scheming designs of its just reappeared owner. Only the next day, when under my mother and grandmother's careful supervision, as they themselves stood on that terrace, did I venture slowly into the garden. And only then, the policeman's wife and another of the women who had settled in one of the ground floor apartments, ventured smilingly in my direction and offered me something sweet to eat.

The adventure seemed to have come to an end. Or had it?

9.
Incipit Vita Nuova

What happened after our return home is another story. To get a feel for these moments, it helps to think about the contexts—the broader flow of time—in which they took place. Now it was no longer necessary to hide, to dissimulate, to divert our gaze when someone looked at us inquisitively, to avoid his or her eyes. Nor was it necessary to adjust every so often my idea about who my parents were. Things could be done out in the open, straightforwardly, honestly. But the condition of uncertainty and flux that marked me during the years of the German occupation could not disappear just at the drop of a hat, simply by taking stock of my parents' affection and their constant, unconditional expression of love and support. In retrospect, in April 1945, we returned to normal life. To a certain extent this is how adults looked at things. But what about the children who had lived through the uncertainties of the previous many months? What was normal to them? Where would stability be found? Our experience of the immediate past—our awareness of the flux, of the unexpected twists and turns of life, of surprises that could spring up at any moment—persisted, if only below the surface of consciousness. This state of mind had been grafted onto my personality and would follow me for years. Still, now there was a new question that faced us: was it possible—especially for me—to explore with open eyes our surroundings and with an open mind decipher the world that greeted us that April of 1945? The years that followed were an adventure of discovery: family, school, friends, perhaps most importantly, if ever so slowly, fashioning a sense of self and of imagining my place at home and in the city where I spent the following eleven years.

Perhaps as important as any of these challenges was a task that over time unfolded in my conscience. What was the significance of my and my family's Jewishness? What did it mean to be Jewish in that place and time? Did our Jewishness set me apart from my classmates and other friends, and if so, how? Could one's Jewishness, in the ten or so years after the war, be distinguished from a culture of grief and protest for the wrongs of this world, from the constant commemoration of the dead? Further, what meaning could a child such as myself give to the celebration of the young, from whom, consciously or not, the older folks expected a sort of redemption for the ills their generation had suffered? I well remember my cringing when, for one of the Jewish holidays, perhaps Sukkoth in 1945, one of the near-adults (I well remember her name, but, since she is still alive, I shall spare her the embarrassment of mentioning it) at a hastily constructed Jewish social center, posed a question to the couple of dozen children gathered there, and then, pointing her finger at me asked loudly, "Let's see how good Tony Molho is." Predictably, I froze and showed to everyone there that I knew nothing, about the question asked or about anything else, in short that in that Jewish context I could not pass muster.

For me, the growing consciousness of being a Jew while not fully understanding the significance of our Jewishness was a refrain of my growing up in Salonica. I think my parents were aware of my uncertainty but did nothing to counter it. In the summer of 1952, I was bar mitzvah in a formal ceremony in which I did not have to demonstrate anything more than having learned the Hebrew alphabet, teased out a few words from the Torah, and memorized the necessary prayers and readings. I simply had not learned to read them with the ease that is expected of thirteen-year-old Jewish boys. Neither my father nor my mother was especially religious, and certainly they were not Zionists as many Salonican Jews had become. If they nurtured a certain general sympathy for the State of Israel, their true sentiment was clearly expressed during a conversation in (I think)1952, when a representative of the State of Israel, after dinner at our house, set out to convince my parents to send me to a kibbutz in Israel where I could become, he argued, a true Jew. My mother cut him short: *Nous n'avons pas sauvé Tony des Allemands pour le faire tuer par un Arabe* (We did not save Tony from the Germans to have him killed by an Arab)! Life counts more than ideology.

In this broader realm, my parents followed a well-established, if inchoate family tradition. One of my father's younger brothers, Alberto Molho, born in 1904 just a few years before the passage of Salonica to the Greek state and known by his nom de plume of Napolitan because of his admiration, indeed his love of Italian literature and culture, was a distinguished, marxisant journalist and author in the 1930s of a number of gently ironic anti-Zionist plays, all of them in Ladino. These have been altogether forgotten in Greece, but, since the 1980s, republished and commented upon in Spain and more recently in Israel. In newspaper articles written in Ladino that appeared in Sephardic newspapers as late as the late 1930s, he resignedly accepted the notion that the Greek language was destined to weigh more heavily in the lives of the city's Jews. That sense of an opening or, if one will, the awareness that, in his life, intellectual and cultural bridges were bringing closer to each other Salonica's Jews and Christians, deeply colored Napolitan's thought. Significantly, his few surviving wartime letters to his brothers were written neither in Ladino nor in French but in Greek! In his public writings, his sardonic humor was trained on the conservative, Zionist sympathies of Salonica's prewar Jewish leadership, with his hopes invested not in the defense of Jewish traditions nor, certainly, in that of the Zionist ideology that had gained wide circulation in the city. Rather, what sustained him was a combination of his Marxisant convictions and a vision (call it realistic or practical) that Salonica's Jews were destined to coexist with their Christian compatriots. I wish I had gotten to know Uncle Alberto. But, having escaped to Egypt at the time of the war, where he obtained minor posts

Figure 9.1. *Alberto Molho, 1904–1945, known as Napolitan, journalist, author of theatrical works, and one of my father's five younger brothers.*

in the bureaucracy of the government-in-exile, he returned to Athens in April 1945 where he died immediately afterward from a heart ailment. I have often wondered how he would have faced the realities of postwar Salonica, and how he would have accommodated in the bundle of his ideas the terrible events of the Shoah, and the foundation of the State of Israel.

Call it an ideology, or simply a point of view, my parents' attitude colored my upbringing and my education from 1945 to 1956, when we left for the United States. No question about our being Jews, of course we were, and declared so unhesitatingly. But we were neither very systematic in our observance of religious rituals nor ready to adhere to whatever line—political or not—that was promoted by the leadership of the Israelite (Jewish) community of Salonica. When, shortly after Stalin's death in 1953, an official of the community, perhaps following a line suggested by the city's US Consulate, equated Stalin's crimes with those of Hitler, my father, at home and in private conversations with friends, strongly disputed that view: how could you compare those two? His views changed after 1956, but this change was as much due to our move to the United States as to the revelations of Stalin's crimes.

My schooling was entrusted entirely to nonreligious schools, where I was immersed in Greek culture and made friends, nearly all of them Christian or at least nominally so. I spent the mornings of my elementary school years in a good, private Greek school, chosen by my parents, I think, for its lukewarm enforcement of the state's religiously colored curriculum. For this reason, my parents did not insist that I be exempted from the obligatory religious lessons (one or two hours a week), which unquestioningly followed, in matters of dogma and of politics, the diktats of the Greek Orthodox Church. In the afternoons,

I was enrolled in an excellent French school, sponsored by the Mission Laïque Française, located at the end of our street a few doors from our house. There, in addition to learning French pretty well, I was indoctrinated into the ideology of the French state. More than once my essays on the meaning of *Libérté, Egalité, Fraternité* won prizes in class, and once, I think in sixth grade, in the school-wide competition. The lessons at school were systematically reinforced at home (or perhaps I should write the opposite, the lessons I picked up at home were reinforced at school). A standard after-dinner question posed by my father to me and whichever of my friends and uncles happened to be around was this: "Why is the French Revolution the greatest event in human history?" His unequivocal and solemnly pronounced answer was that "thanks to the French Revolution, when Tony grows up and applies for a job, no one will ask him who his father is, or whom he knows. Employers will simply want to find out what he knows and is able to do." That was the real meaning of equality, a deeply held value for my father, and his brothers.

When I reached the age of twelve, in 1951, I was enrolled in the boys' section of Anatolia College, a school that my mother and her sister attended in the 1930s. Anatolia, as all of us simply called it, had been founded by US Protestant missionaries in Merzifun in Asia Minor and was transferred to Salonica following the massive Greek defeat in the Greek-Turkish war in 1922. There, in the hinterland of Asia Minor and in northern Greece, US missionaries transferred their mixture of rigorous Midwestern American Protestantism, which they adjusted to the peculiarities of local cultures—Greek, Armenian, and Jewish, whose members represented the bulk of their student enrollments. In 1951, I arrived at the school's boys division as an internal student, sleeping in the dormitory six nights a week and going home from early Saturday afternoon to early Sunday evening, in other words ordinarily missing Shabbat observance. The school followed the curriculum of the Greek Ministry of Education, except that some classes—Science, Music History, Social Studies, and of course English literature—were held in English. At school, I continued my study of the piano, thanks to my music teacher, Madame Abravanel, who to my classmates' amusement and their intermittent bantering, continued to come to the school once or twice a week to follow my progress in piano and music theory. Then, after the second year, in coincidence with my discovery of "serious" music, a veritable *coup de foudre* for me, I convinced my parents to allow me to return home and continue at Anatolia as an external student. I argued that it was easier to follow from home the city's musical life, which was being revived by fits and starts in postwar Salonica. In fact, I did so assiduously for the last three or more years, until our departure for the United States, where, thanks to Georges Szell and the Cleveland Orchestra's magical spell on me, I even toyed with the idea of abandoning my studies and becoming a musician.

At school, I had some excellent teachers, who, on the surface at least, almost entirely overlooked my Jewishness, and developed deep friendships with classmates, some of which have lasted to this day. In my dealings with these friends, I never had the impression that my Jewishness was an issue. Significantly, not one of them ever asked for details about my family's and my survival during the war. Nor, strangely, did I, even once, feel the need to explain to them what had happened to me and to my family. More recently, I often asked myself if we were not all acting on the basis of a mutually understood, but never explicit, consensus of silence about the war: they did not wish to single me out by exposing my otherness, and I did not dwell on aspects of my background that distinguished me from them nor did I wish to raise the delicate issues of collaboration and of the fate of Jewish properties in wartime and postwar Salonica. I participated in many sports and after-school activities, and was subjected to the friendly, mostly harmless bullying that was typical of boys' sociability in those years. Only once, as I remember, did someone fling the word "Jew" at me as an insult. This was when I was still a boarder. For reasons I do not remember, I returned to our dorm late in the evening after everyone was already in bed and the lights had been turned off. As I was fumbling in the dark trying to get to my bed, I stumbled and heard one of the boys loudly curse me with a pejorative expression often used in Greece against Jews. Someone else shouted to him to shut up because he was trying to sleep and the case was closed.

Two incidents, both of them in my last year at the school, suggest that, however implicit, the issue of my Jewishness lay dormant just slightly below everyone's behavior, mine, my friends', even my teachers' and the school's administration. In my case, the lines of demarcation between Jewishness and Christianity (which in those days was equivalent to Greekness) had been attenuated, sometimes they were invisible, but they were still there and served the purpose of singling me out from the group.

Although the school had a boys' and a girls' section, classes, sports, even school buses and most extracurricular activities were strictly segregated. But there were a few occasions, especially sports events when girls were allowed to stand on the sidelines cheering for the boys' (usually excellent) sports teams, with boys reciprocating in girls' sports competitions. There

Figure 9.2. *School excursion. I am sitting second from right. Sitting wearing a baseball cap, our American teacher Mr. Yoder (But I am unsure if this was his name!), 1955–1956.*

were also some extracurricular clubs when the separation of the genders was not strictly enforced. Somewhere in the school, I had spotted a girl, my age, and incidentally also Jewish, who struck my fancy. I guessed that my chance of seeing her more often, perhaps even of talking with her—a very daring thought at the time—might be the creation of one of these extracurricular clubs where students could discuss issues of Jewish interest. Little did I know the reaction that would follow, a veritable storm! I submitted my petition to the teacher responsible for such after-school activities, who, unbeknownst to me, passed it on to the school president, Dr. Carl Compton, who in turn consulted the Chairman of the Board of Trustees in Boston! All of them, without ever asking me, assumed that my initiative was inspired by some American Jewish organization, and its intention was to create a Zionist cell on campus. A few weeks after submitting my petition, I was called to the president's office and was told that my request had been denied. I was confronted by a couple of administrators and one or two teachers. They very calmly explained that the school did not allow the creation of religiously based organizations and for this reason they could not approve my petition. At the time I was not very upset, as I had already started fantasizing about another possible girlfriend, who, incidentally, was not Jewish. But I did not mention anything about this at home, for fear of my parents' reaction, which would almost certainly have been to forget about girls and concentrate on my studies. Years later, I laughed at the whole incident. Boy wants to meet girl, who in any case is not even aware of the boy's existence. But to trigger such a reaction from Salonica to Boston! Would a request from one of my classmates to create a club where to discuss the lives of the Church Fathers have produced the same reaction? I suspect not. Being Jewish was important! In certain matters, it could be a determining factor.

This was also the point of the second event I remember. But that incident was no laughing matter. It left a deep mark on me; from the moment it happened, I took it as a symbolic slap on the face. The event's protagonist was one of my favorite teachers, who also seemed to like me. After my move to the United States, he took the initiative to write to me, and for a few years, I corresponded with him, informing him of my studies and progress. He was an undogmatic, mild-mannered, and open-minded man of the left and a highly accomplished scholar, having been awarded significant prizes from learned societies in Greece for his distinguished philological studies. All these considerations conspired to shock me at his reaction to something I told him.

COURAGE AND COMPASSION

In my last year at Anatolia, he asked me about my plans for university studies and professional ambitions. My plan, I said, was to study political science and aim for a career in the Greek diplomatic service. To this day, his reaction reverberates in my mind. I think I remember very clearly his words as he uttered them, squeezed as we were in his tiny study. Forget it, he responded softly. They do not take Jews in the Ministry of Foreign Affairs. I said nothing and left his office shaken. In this instance too, I did not mention anything to my parents, but this time because I was too ashamed of my teacher for bringing out into the open such an offensive comment.

But that night, alone in my room, I cried. Anger, disappointment, and my sense of alienation were too powerful to control. By then, I had read a French translation of Anne Frank's Diary, that we had discussed more than once at home, and I had seen newsreels and read books about the Third Reich and about Auschwitz. I knew an anti-Jewish comment when I heard one. I might have expected such a comment from some other teachers. But from him? Many years later, my late wife, who was Jewish, suggested that perhaps I had exaggerated the import of that moment. Perhaps my teacher simply wanted to prepare me for unpleasant reactions to my professional plans from university professors and state functionaries. He tried to help you, not to hurt you, she said. Perhaps. But without a question, I took it as my most painful moment at Anatolia, perhaps of my entire adolescence. That conversation helped to greatly mute my initial opposition to my mother's determination that we leave Greece and move to the United States. Why should I want to leave my friends, the fabulous summers at the YMCA camp in the idyllic village of Saint John on Mount Pylion, and be separated from my beloved grandmother, my uncles, aunts, and cousins? The conversation with that teacher, which could not have lasted more than five or six minutes, drove the point home, as nothing that had happened to me until then. I realized how unbridgeable were some lines that separated me from my friends in Greece. I would go along with my mother and father's plans to seek my luck elsewhere, in a land I thought I knew from movies and books, where, my mother had insisted, Jews were treated as equals, and discrimination against them did not exist.

As so often in my life, surprises were not long in coming. In mid- to late 1950s Ohio, I was profoundly struck by my discovery of Ashkenazi Jews, of their language, rituals, and traditions. They shared little with the middle-class world of Jewish Salonica I knew; their customs seemed alien, even crude, and offensive in many East European Jews' apparent condescension toward Jews from different traditions. Initially I was deeply disoriented. Did I thus become more sensitive to my double Greek and Jewish background? I suspect not. At least initially, what happened was that I began to identify myself as American, with rather faded hues both of my Greek and Jewish backgrounds present in my mind. New lines of demarcation now began to orient my life. Then, at the end of my third year at college, I was turned down for a summer job for which I had applied at the East 105th Street YMCA in Cleveland. Having spent endless hours in the Salonica YMCA without ever a question raised about whether I was fit for the institution, it never occurred to me that in the United States, an infinitely more liberal and open society as I certainly thought, my Jewishness would create a problem. But it did, and it was made clear to me that as a Jew I would not be qualified to hold a position at the Cleveland Young Men's Christian Association summer camp. Welcome to America!

Figure 9.3. *Bazaar at Anatolia College, I stand fifth from left, 1955.*

For me, the time from our return to Salonica in 1945 to our departure eleven years later was a period of discovery and adjustment to new and surprising but largely not unpleasant circumstances. For my parents, often bitterly disappointing surprises marked those years. It was a time of huge challenges. Before, the challenge had been to survive—to hide and blend themselves unnoticed in the background, even to carve for each one of themselves a new identity. Now, the challenge was to construct something new and strive to return to a condition of normality. They had had their wish and managed to return home. But the odds against their success were immense. In fact, for them, life never returned to normal, whatever "normal" could have meant under those circumstances. My mother struggled to come to terms with the empty spaces in her life. For my father, quiet, at times taciturn as he was, the most immediate task was to provide for his family and to rebuild his business. The challenge consumed him, and I cannot remember him being relaxed and cheerful, except perhaps during his weekly day-long treks through the mountains around Salonica. He never was in a bad mood, just serious and preoccupied.

For him, a large part of his routine was traveling—by public transport, as we never had a car—in the provincial cities and villages of Macedonia and Thrace, in an attempt to rebuild his clientele (tailors and small-scale clothes merchants). I do not know how successful he was in his business, but his honesty and trustworthiness made him popular with his customers. When he departed for Cleveland, he left a large number of accounts that, for one reason or another, his customers could not pay. In 1962, I first returned to Salonica and went on a tour to collect some of his customers' debts. I was warmly greeted with sweets, ouzo, and coffee by everyone I visited, but I collected very little cash. A sign of the times, my lack of business acumen, or merely the way my father had set up his business? Shortly after his death in Cleveland in March 1967, my mother received a mass of letters from people she had not ever met or even heard of. They had been his customers, who even more than ten years following our departure from Greece, remembered him and wrote with fondness and great respect for him.

In the first few years following the war, I recall three occasions that teased out of my father, once again, traits of his prewar charming and attractive personality that had made him a pleasant companion to friends and acquaintances. The experience of the Shoah had changed him, not as evidently as it had my mother. But in his quieter and more pensive way, his disposition had become darker and more pessimistic, more inclined to look at the less promising outcomes of ventures he might undertake. A birth and two weddings showed me a side of my father I rarely observed as I was growing up. The family was now trying to renew its energies, it was facing aspects of life that had been overlooked, even forgotten in the preceding years.

I think his greatest pleasure after the war came with my sister Marcella's birth more than a year after our return to Evzonon Street. No question that Marcella's arrival to our house was at once a direct outcome of the war and of the Shoah, while also marking an important, if not clean break from our wartime experiences. In the months following April 1945, my mother suffered a breakdown, took to her bed, and essentially passed the summer months confined to her room. A regular visitor to our house in that period was Dr. Vaïnanidis (my namesake!), always arriving in his horse-drawn buggy that he would tie to our garden's entrance, often entrusting the horse to my care, even for long stretches of time. He usually had lunch with us. After examining my mother, he and my father would step out to the terrace for coffee. On one of these occasions, I remember overhearing a conversation between them. I did not understand the meaning of the exchange, but I remember all too well what the doctor said. It must have been in July or August 1946, very shortly after my sister's birth, on 3 July. Dr. Vaïnanidis reassured my father. Your wife will be saved by your daughter, he said. Later my mother told me that it was he, our family doctor, who had insisted with my father that my parents try to have another child. He proved to be right.

Marcella's presence brought a new dynamic to our house. Slowly, if only intermittently, the horrors of the Shoah were gradually overshadowed in my mother's mind. From the moment of her birth, through her years of maturity in the United States when she became Head Mistress of a prestigious private

Figure 9.4. *With my mother and sister Marcella, born on 3 July 1946. The photograph was taken in the autumn of 1946.*

school in Maryland, until Marcella's very sadly premature death a few years ago, my kid sister demanded attention! The need to tend to the newly arrived member of the family forced my mother to concentrate on the present and the future and to focus less on her losses. But not even her daughter's birth could distract my mother from her overriding desire to leave the city and change the surroundings in which she lived. She succeeded in that goal, by leaving Greece and moving with the family to Cleveland, Ohio.

For my father, *papà* for my sister, this little girl's presence in our lives was a fantastic energizer. Needless to say, Marcella ran circles around him, always managing to get him to do favors for her, while he, invariably, did all he could to please her. In the summer of 1951, when my mother and I visited her Uncle Albert in Constantinople (Istanbul) for a month, father and five-year-old daughter were left alone at home under the vigilant supervision of my sister's nanny and a cook. The two of them seem to have had a grand time, even though my mother, upon our return to Salonica, scolded him more than once because during that month Marcella had abandoned all discipline and good manners! Years later I also discovered that daughters (and I have had three!) have a way of getting around their disciplinarian mothers by forming alliances with their fathers . . .

Not a year had passed since Marcella's birth, when my two uncles' weddings offered triumphant confirmation of everyone's passionate desire to return to some sort of normality. These weddings lingered on in my memory, both because of my father's role in them and of the deep impressions that both events left on me, as well as the questions about them that for years lingered in my mind.

I remember very well my father's role in Uncle Roufa's and Aunt Henrietta's wedding in 1947. Roufa (Raphael) had become Nicos during the war and interestingly had retained that name even after the war, especially among some relatives and close friends. This was the uncle who was always in good humor and told me funny stories; during our years of hiding in Athens, he once took me for a long walk to the center of the city to show me some of the important sites. Their wedding was a very special occasion. My future aunt had returned from Auschwitz psychologically a wreck, with the tattoo of a number on her left arm—a decoration or blemish that she carried for life but which she steadfastly refused to comment on until perhaps more than four decades after returning to Salonica from the concentration camp. Thanks to her radiant personality, once she was at home, she managed to bounce back and soon thereafter accepted her prewar beau's, my Uncle Roufa's, proposal for marriage. Roufa had chosen to marry his sweetheart with whom he had flirted before the war. She was very poor but very beautiful. They were in love, were lucky to survive, and married because they wanted each other. Contrarily to the case of my parents or to other close relatives, there was no talk of dowries, marriage contracts, or property exchanges between them. More than once afterward, *Yiayià* Flora would recount how very pleased she had been when Roufa, the youngest of her seven children, asked her permission to marry Henrietta. (His version was somewhat different. He had not asked for permission, he insisted. He had simply

Figure 9.5. *Wedding photograph of Uncle Raphael (Roufa) and Aunt Henrietta, 1947; she had returned from Auschwitz about two years earlier.*

informed her. Big difference!) Too poor to buy herself a wedding dress, my future aunt wore a tailored two-piece suit borrowed from a friend, and a simple white veil, and held a small bouquet given her by her future husband.

Their wedding was the first important family reunion after the war, and I remember it vividly, even if I do not recall a ceremony at the synagogue, because the marriage ritual was most probably held in my grandmother's house. But the reception that followed was a different matter, I remember it all too well. It, also, was held at my grandmother's house in the presence of the Molhos, of my aunt's few surviving relatives, and a handful of friends. After a rabbi recited some prayers in a language—Hebrew—that entirely puzzled me, my father, now the senior male member of the family, invited the beautiful bride for the evening's first dance, a waltz, to the music of an accordion and a fiddle engaged, as I remember, by my father. I can now see myself, sprawled on the floor under the dining room table that had been pushed to the side to make room for the dancers, peeking half embarrassed–half enthusiastic and wondering what that was all about. My father dancing! Who had ever heard of that? And what was dancing all about? Never heard of it before. Then, everyone danced—mostly the waltz and the tango, but not once, as I remember, Greek folk dances. The newlyweds danced, then my parents, Uncle Isaac and the bridegroom with their mother, then with my mother, my father with his mother, all the while I remained an observer to this magical, happy scene, transported to another universe of sheer satisfaction and pleasure. That evening's magic lived on in my mind for years. And I registered clearly my father's standing as the head of this large and apparently happy family.

At the time, perhaps inevitably, I could not even imagine the emotions that were swirling on that improvised dance floor.

What were Henrietta's thoughts—not so much her thoughts as her feelings? She had spent two years in an infernal corner of northern Europe; lived every day there as if it were her last, forced to survive on potato peelings and bits of garbage, every ounce of her spare energy consumed by an unceasing torment about parents, family and friends; and now, here she was laughing at the indescribable joy of the moment, knowing that she was back in the safety of her old home, dancing with her husband to the tune of a waltz, as everyone's eyes were fixed on her, with every refrain of the music creating more confusion in her mind. Was it all real? Was this really happening to her? Was there a way to balance in her mind her two recent experiences? The utter despair of Auschwitz, the sheer bliss of that moment. Of course, not one of these thoughts crossed my mind that evening. But this was the substance of a conversation Henrietta had with my mother about three years later. I had been sick and stayed in bed with some sort of a cold, and Aunt Henrietta had come to visit me. My mother was perched at the edge of my bed, my aunt on a chair nearby and the two started a long discussion, while I was drifting in and out of sleep. Alberto, Henrietta and Roufa's firstborn given the name of Napolitan, my journalist uncle who had died immediately after the war, had been born more than a year earlier, and Henrietta now softly told my mother that she "could not hide it anymore," she was pregnant again. Then, she launched in a long confession, half understood by me, about her powerful emotions since her return to Salonica. With every passing day, her life in Salonica was becoming increasingly real. But from the time of her return until her marriage she was uncertain about the reality of it all. The tattooed number on her left arm would not let her forget, even for a moment, the reality of that horrible experience.

Figure 9.6. With my sister, Marcella, at Uncle Isaac and Aunt Rita's wedding, 1949.

Many years later, perhaps toward the end of the 1980s, I heard for the first time the mesmerizing, intense ballad written by Leonard Cohen, the Canadian troubadour who spent several months each year in his house in the island of Hydra in the Aegean Sea. "Dance Me to the End of Love," sang the composer's gravelly, passionate voice. I was deeply moved by the music and the lyrics. Then, not long ago, I discovered that Cohen composed this song in memory of a twenty-year-old pregnant Jewish woman from Salonica, who was led to the crematorium at Auschwitz as her husband, Jacques Stroumsa, himself from Salonica and a prisoner at the *Lager*, was playing first violin in a Jewish orchestra commandeered by the Germans at the camp. And I wondered if, more than a Strauss waltz, the Canadian troubadour's notes might not have been a more fitting accompaniment to Aunt Henrietta's wedding celebration. But none of this mattered to me while at the age of eight I was sprawled under the dining room table at my grandmother's house taking in the dream-like spectacle of the dancers swirling round and round an arm's length from me.

The moment was sealed in my mind that evening, it was one of the most powerful memories of my childhood. As years passed, a thorn-like question, like a weed, grew next to that image, pricking my conscience, violently upsetting the balance and beauty of that scene: how was it that one woman, after a harrowing trip from Salonica to Poland and back, managed to arrive to her wedding day dancing to one of Johann Strauss's famous tunes, while another, perhaps a friend or acquaintance in Salonica, perished in the *Lager* at such a young age and now, so many years after her death, was commemorated by a famous Canadian song writer who had never known her. As Mr. Stroumsa explained to an interviewer many years later, chance, the chance of a gesture of an impassive German soldier, determined if his wife would survive or not. You go left and you live. You are ordered to turn right, and you die. The question has turned round and round endlessly in my mind, more than once keeping me awake at night. I guess it is because it is comparable to the question I ask myself about my and my parents' survival.

Two years later, it was Uncle Isaac's turn to get married. During the war, he had become Yannis, but he shed that name almost immediately after his return home. He was the one of the small chalk gifts during my stretch at Vizyinou Street. Following

Figure 9.7. *Uncle Isaac's and Aunt Rita's wedding in 1949, with my sister Marcella, aged three, as flower girl.*

his return to Salonica, he lived, first with us, and then moved with his mother into her beautiful, if somewhat cramped, apartment on the corniche. I have no idea if his unattached condition bothered him, but it almost certainly agitated other members of the family. Just as a joint effort was launched to correct Isaac's situation, Rita Matalon appeared on the horizon. It was the right moment. She and my mother had known each other from their prewar days at the State Conservatory of Music. From a once very affluent family, she had managed to survive the occupation by remaining hidden for about a year and a half in a small basement apartment in Athens, never, not even once according to her, leaving her confinement. Perhaps because of that traumatic experience she had become somewhat awkward in her social habits and even after the war when she was well into her thirties, she had remained, as one used to say, unattached.

Sometime in 1948, shortly after her return from the years of hiding in Athens, while on a stroll in the center of Salonica, my mother ran into her. They had not seen each other for years, and they started catching up with their news. Almost immediately, my mother rose to the challenge: here was a youngish, unmarried, handsome woman from a "good" family with ample means. Why not find out if her own brother-in-law, my Uncle Isaac, himself not in his first youth, might be interested in marrying her? Rita was asked on the spot if she would allow my mother to make such an inquiry. She had no objection and, to make a long story short, a few weeks later, their engagement was officially marked at our house after an elaborate and, as I remember, endless Sunday lunch attended by all the Molhos and Rita's mother. My father, because he was the oldest male Molho present, proposed, in Ladino and in French, a toast for the future newlyweds, and I was allowed, for the first time ever, to take a sip of wine so that, as my father whispered to me, I could wish Uncle Isaac and soon-to-be Aunt Rita a happy and long life. Then, we all went on a nice country walk, with me, nudged by Uncle Roufa and my parents, walking ahead with Isaac and Rita on either side of me! Nice role I had been given. Make sure that the couple—she in her mid-thirties, he close to fifty—would enjoy each other's company all the while being supervised by a nine-year-old charged with ensuring that they would neither touch nor say something untoward to each other!

Soon after, Isaac and Rita were married in an elaborate and impressive ceremony. He had arranged for a taxi, wonderfully decorated with white flowers (I think they were lilies and carnations, as I can now see in a very nice picture of Marcella and me, who accompanied the newlyweds to the synagogue) and on his way to meet Rita at her house, he stopped to pick me up, so that, I suppose, escort and overseer that I had been in their previous encounters, I would also accompany them now to the synagogue. The stop at Rita's house gave me occasion to hear for the first time a comment I heard Isaac repeat to Rita many times in later years. *Addiò Rita, dépêches-toi, nous serons en retard.* We drove to the synagogue, where my father was second man to his brother, then on to a nice restaurant, and from there the newlyweds went on to a seaside resort near Athens for their honeymoon.

On these occasions—his two brothers' weddings—not to mention my sister's arrival in our family, I had the chance to see firsthand my father's more relaxed and smiling persona. Generally, as I said, he was deeply absorbed by his affairs, intent as he almost always was to ensure that his business would enable him to support his family at a level he considered appropriate. Then, starting around 1950, he took on the pro bono work as president of an organization charged with determining the fate of Jewish properties in Salonica. So many of their owners had been murdered in concentration camps that tangled questions about proper heirs had to be sorted out. I remember my father often returning home late in the evening, having first spent a full workday in his business and then attended a two- or three-hour meeting to discuss inheritance questions and try to reconcile often heated disputes among potential heirs.

His business and his other activities absorbed him almost entirely, and he had little time left for me. I am sorry I never grew close to him, taking his shyness and seriousness as either disinterest or disapproval of me. Not that there was any friction between us. I knew that he expected me to be a good student and not to "get into trouble." I do not think I gave him any occasion to disappoint him, at least not while we stayed in Salonica. Then, in the United States, I did my best to readjust the balance between us and did all I could, it seems, to offend his sense of propriety. Yet, time and again, his generosity and his unshakable sense of family solidarity surprised, even moved me. He died on 21 March 1967, a few days after suffering a stroke. By then I had myself become a father and was at the beginning of my teaching career. We had started talking to each other more extensively and, I think, maturely only a few years before. After he died, I realized that, as I was growing up, I had done him a great injustice by misjudging his quiet and shy personality as a studied disinterest toward me. That was not true. But it was too late for me to correct this wrong.

Perhaps most crucially, I never had the chance to acknowledge my gratitude for his immense sacrifice to leave Greece and move to the United States, a country in which he never really felt at home, one that he accepted reluctantly and only with great uncertainty. He had yielded to my mother's insistence (and dare I add, to her egoism) and—at an age, he was fifty-seven when we left Salonica, when changes of this sort are not easy to contemplate—gave up his languages, his customs, his standing in a society he knew well, his mother, and his brothers to jump into an adventure that, in retrospect it was easy to foresee, would not have a happy ending for him. Were it not for his immediate family—which did its best to complicate his life—the United States for Saul Molho, eldest son of Lazar Molho and of Flora Hasson, born in the very distant year 1899 in a city that was itself very distant not only geographically, was worse than unpleasant—it was a nightmare, for all his effort to put a good face to it and appear satisfied with his children's successes. A proud and reasonably accomplished entrepreneur, whom his acquaintances esteemed and invariably treated with respect and admiration, now became a manual worker, feeling degraded because of this painful process of downward mobility. For his children—my sister and me—the transition was a series of challenges, which, I think, we overcame reasonably successfully. My mother flourished in her new environment. Her age—she was forty-one at the time of our move—her more dynamic and gregarious personality, her fierce determination, her decision to cultivate her skills in the world of learning and education all helped her emerge in her new life as a successful and much-admired teacher and academic administrator. Within eight years of our arrival in Cleveland, she obtained her college degree, a master's degree, and a doctorate. How many women in the immediate post-Eisenhower US society had the ambition and self-discipline to aim professionally so high and successfully attain their goals? But for my father, his transplantation to a new world produced mostly the bitter fruit of disappointment and a sense of failure. For him, and for my family more widely, the Shoah had consequences that extended not years but decades into the peace that followed the war. In the distorted and iniquitous logic of our family's history, his disappointments and failure were part and parcel of the rest of the family's success. As I mentioned in the preceding chapter, I have the nagging suspicion that my mother's return to Salonica in the 1980s may not have been unrelated to her increasingly acute sense of guilt toward my father. How could she have done this to him? Could she continue living in a place where she was constantly reminded that my father could survive only for ten years the trauma of his transition to this *mondus novus*?

Figure 9.8. *My mother on the day she received her doctorate (Ph.D.) degree at Western Reserve University in Cleveland, Ohio, 1964.*

COURAGE AND COMPASSION

I remember twice, in my earlier years, when I yearned for time to stop so I could continue living just as I was doing then. The first time was when I was fourteen. At the time, life was altogether satisfactory: music, sports, friends, reading, dream-like summers in what I knew to be one of the most beautiful spots on earth, the first premonitions of an interest in girls, not to speak of *Yiayià* Flora, uncles, and aunts. Life held so many pleasures. That bubble of dream-like, frozen time lived on in my mind for many years, even after my life had taken a decidedly different turn. I remember, several years later, stopping to ask myself what was my preferred age. Invariably, the answer was fourteen! The experiences of my recent hiding—after all, it had been less than ten years before—had slowly receded in my mind, the complexion of those moments had faded away, just like old, yellowed pictures you squint at through a thin and opaque time-worn veil gently deposited on them. The picture in my first police ID card taken when I was fourteen years old, shows my happy, clean-cut, baby-like face (as my friends at school used to tease me), at peace with the world. There was a dissonant note on that ID, but I was not bothered by it, assuming I even noticed it at the time. The entry of religious affiliation stated that I was Jewish. Big deal! Did being Jewish have an importance in my life? In my teens, it did not seem to me that it did. Without much thinking about it, within eight years of our return to Evzonon Street, I had found a balance in my life. My past had been nudged into the background; it had stopped interfering with my life.

Then, in my thirties, I had a comparable feeling. By then, I had resolved the issue of my Jewishness, acknowledging, to myself and to others, that this part of my existence had taken its just place in my consciousness. Being Jewish was one of the

TONY MOLHO

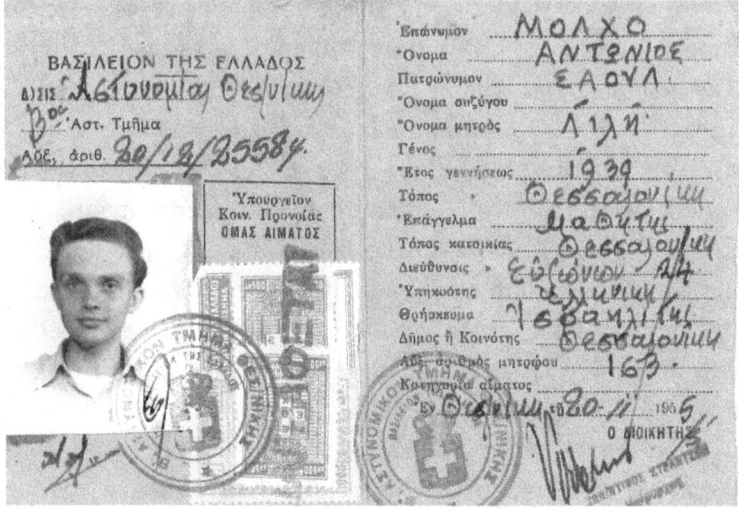

Figure 9.9. *My police ID, 1955.*

sides of my being, certainly not the only one, but a side that I readily acknowledged for its importance and did not want to overlook. Shortly after my arrival in Providence, Rhode Island, the wife of one of my senior colleagues advised me to avoid looking for housing in a certain neighborhood because it was inhabited mostly by Jews. At first, I hesitated, frozen in uncertainty on how to respond. After all, I had only recently arrived for my new teaching position, her husband was a real academic boss, powerful and ever ready to impose his point of view, while I was an untenured, precarious twenty-seven-year-old teacher. But after a few moments, speaking vigorously to her, I gave my first, if informal, lecture in my new position: a brief overview of the history and importance of Sephardic Judaism. The reasons for my pleasure during those years were different. My discovery and passionate engagement with Italy and with historical research, the birth of my two daughters, a teaching position with

Figure 9.10. *At Brown University, summer 1966.*

a salary decent enough to provide for my family, and a splendid group of colleagues and friends throughout North America and Europe. Once again, I yearned for time to stop. Could I not continue living in that happy condition? It turns out, I could not.

Surprises kept popping up. One of these amused and startled me. In my early forties, when I was head of my department, I accidentally discovered that an official document of my department's ethnic and racial profile to my astonishment included one Hispanic person. I could not understand. Who was this Hispanic colleague? The department secretary soon shed light on the mystery. It turns out that one of the previous heads, having been required by the university administration to compile such a profile, had decided to list me as Hispanic! Shortly thereafter, I confronted him, and he very apologetically explained that my Sephardic Jewishness suggested that my ancestry had originated in the Iberian Peninsula, hence I was Hispanic! No matter that by the term "Hispanic" the administration had in mind what, today, one refers to as Latino. No, I was not Hispanic; I was Jewish. At that moment, I came to realize that one's Jewishness could make itself felt in unpredictable and surprising ways.

Figure 9.11. *With my mother, a few weeks before her death in August 2006.*

10.
After the End

Someone—I do not now remember who—is once supposed to have said that it might take longer than a lifetime to explain a life. I don't know anything about explaining a life. But it surely took me a very long time to present these few memories of a two-year stretch of time. But explain? How to explain them, assuming I knew how to define to my satisfaction what I mean by "explain" in this context. Is it possible to wrest meaning from these dabs of memory so many years after the events they evoke? And what meaning should I try to unearth in them? Meaning about these memories when they were first formed? I rather doubt that, drawing on my childhood adventures, I could say anything about the Shoah that has not already been said, often with understated eloquence and force by others. Or meaning about smaller places—Salonica, Athens, Greece—or shorter times (my life, the lives of my parents and relatives)? The incommensurability between the small scale of one child's experiences and the immensity of the Shoah is such that "meaning" in one realm would hardly fit in another, even if, perhaps, the temptation might be present. Might the difference in the scale of the two realms help to illuminate both, as an observer casts the shadow of one realm of experience onto the other, thus teasing meaning from a small boy's wartime adventures?

In any case, why should one search for meaning or an explanation? Why should not a forthright presentation do? My answer is simple and straightforward. However much some of my friends might desire that I do just that—write a clear and linear narrative, with a beginning, middle, and end—I am unable to construct and present such a "simple narrative" of what happened to me during the occupation. Because I was so young at the time of these events; because I am often uncertain about the origin of my memories, unable to distinguish between my own, direct memories, and those generally referred to as indirect ones; because, finally, I have learned through the years that "simple narratives," whatever that term might mean, are not especially to my liking, preferring as I do more complex, knotty, analytical if inconclusive, even if occasionally somewhat confusing presentations, ones that often double back onto themselves and cast light on diverse, even contradictory, aspects of things.

Even so, now that I have brought to some sort of closure this process of writing and have read this essay not in bits and pieces, but from beginning to end, questions and uncertainties linger in my mind.

A friend pointed out that Germans are almost entirely absent from my account. He is right, and I ask myself why this is so. After all, the German occupation of Greece and the Germans' fiendish determination to exterminate all Jews living in Greece (and, of course, everywhere else they could) are the indelible facts in the background. True enough, my parents and I succeeded to escape the Germans' maniacal persecution. But should I not have been more struck by the Germans' presence in the places where I was hidden during the war years? Should

COURAGE AND COMPASSION

I not have retained more impressions of the thuggishness of the German occupiers or of the duplicity and dishonesty of local collaborators? Of course, the two German soldiers billeted in Evzonon Street did leave an impression on me, despite my very young age. But their appearance was fleeting, even if their actions left a deep imprint on my mother and retrospectively on me. In later years, occasionally I wondered who they were and what happened to them. Recently, I read of a German soldier who deserted his army unit while serving in Greece, joined the partisans, fought with them against his compatriots, and after the war settled in East Germany where he died. Might he have been one of the two who lived with us for a while? I doubt it. I suspect that more such honorable Germans came through Greece during the war years, but of course I would not have had the chance to see or meet them after we left Salonica.

The fact that my memories of those years contain no traces of German soldiers, or more generally of a German presence, suggests to me that, in Salonica as in Athens, I was at once unusually lucky and effectively insulated from danger. It was as if an invisible protective wall surrounded me all along, from the time of *Mamà* Elpida and *Babàs* Yiorgos's house in Salonica in the spring of 1943, to those two anonymous men who, in all likelihood, saved the day in late summer and winter of 1944–45: the remarkably courageous passenger in the tram who thrust himself in the line of danger to allow my mother to escape a police dragnet and the owner of the building who rushed out to the street to beckon us to the safety of his home when, stunned, we were caught in the middle of shooting in late December 1944 or early January 1945. For twenty-five or so months, without much of an effort on my part, I found myself in one or another safe place. No credit here goes to me. On one or two occasions while hiding, I had been warned to stay quiet so as not to make my presence known to others. But to me, this was hardly more than a game. At no time, do I think, was I conscious of the stakes involved. In contrast to the meticulous planning of the Jews' extermination, in Salonica and elsewhere, for me the game ended as it did by chance, a good roll of the dice. It just happened, as if a combination of circumstances, created by the daring of others, led to my survival. Of course, the daring of others was crucial. But I could hardly take credit for that. It takes a miracle for a baby to grow into old age, so many things could go wrong along the way. So, mused an early sixteenth-century historian whose thought has fascinated me since I first discovered his writings in the spring of 1963. I wonder what Francesco Guicciardini might have made of my adventures and survival during the terrible years of Greece's German occupation.

Sometimes I wonder if my knowledge of our success to survive might account for the occasionally self-satisfied, perhaps even nostalgic tone of bits of the preceding presentation. The fact of the matter is that I almost never thought back on these experiences angrily. Nor have I held a grudge for the loss of presumably precious childhood experiences, or for the privations that I, together with the vast majority of Jewish children in Europe, and of nearly all children in Greece, suffered because of the war and the German occupation. And the almost incalculable economic losses suffered by my family during the war never registered with me when I was a kid. Yet, as the years passed, I could not help but wonder what course our lives might have taken if my father's and my grandfather's businesses had not been devastated as a result of German confiscations and of the treacherous activities of presumed Greek friends. To be sure, I often fantasized about the chance to have known Nissim

COURAGE AND COMPASSION

and Henrietta Alkalay, my maternal grandparents, *Oncle* Richard, *Tante* Marcelle, my cousins and other relatives who never returned from Auschwitz. No doubt that this brutal break in family continuity violates my sense of who I am. But my incredibly generous and humane Molho grandmother, *Yiayià* Flora, enveloped me with her love and support for all the years following my return to Salonica, making me feel protected and loved. I can honestly, if very sadly, confess that in the immediate aftermath of the war, I did not miss my murdered relatives. Their large photographic portraits hanging on our living room walls were constant reminders of their existence and of their importance in my ancestral past. But, only years after the war, did I become aware of the very significant if abrupt and violent familial mutilation conveyed by these photographs. The experience of the war itself did not give rise to any such a sentiment.

I have now traveled back to the beginning, in fact to two beginnings. The beginning of my adventure to a long-vanished world almost eighty years ago, when I was not quite four years old; and the beginning of recording these adventures, less than one year ago, although my fumbling efforts to understand what this exercise would entail stretches back to perhaps ten years or more. But the writing itself was squeezed into a few months, when, immobilized by the pandemic that was afflicting us, I was mostly confined to my apartment in Athens. "In moments of stillness, one's mind will step with disconcerting ease into the past," mused a contemporary English intellectual. I think he is right. My mind stepped into my past, and this stepping back led me to start recording these memories. Thanks to this exercise, I now have in my mind images—often sharply etched images—of people, of conversations, of scenes, even of colors, and sounds that, if they had survived at all before, had done so dimly and confusedly, ungraspable shadows that unexpectedly slipped in and out of my consciousness. Now, many of these shadows have taken human forms: people who appear and reappear before my eyes, beckoning me to remember them, to acknowledge their presence in my life. The time that elapsed between these two beginnings can be measured in decades. Yet, the time of these memories is immeasurable and ungraspable; it is a volatile time, constantly changing. At times, even, its contradictory movements are simultaneously present in my mind, frozen, as it were, into a composite and multilayered time, my five-year-old persona and my eighty-three-year-old present self, superimposed on the other, each at once reciprocally illuminating and concealing the other. It is a time that at once enriches the past, while transforming the present. And it does not stop. It did not stop in March 1943 nor, certainly, did it stop following April 1945.

I am starting to put the finishing touches on this small book on 27 January 2022. Today is the day when, the world over, the Shoah is commemorated. The coincidence strikes me as interesting, but I take it to be no more than a coincidence. More than once, my mother had expressed her hope that I write a book of this sort, so I could recount some of our own adventures, which are an integral but tiny fragment of the Shoah. I suspect she would have been at once pleased and irritated by what I wrote. I have no doubt that my father would have been rather pleased, keeping to himself whatever objections might have come up in his mind. Had they been alive today, I would have presented it to them with great pleasure not devoid, I confess, of some anxiety. My mother, who was more of an extrovert and more talkative than my father might have wondered: Did I reveal too many family secrets than others should know? Did I overlook matters of greater importance than those I wrote about? Should

I not have dwelled more extensively on my father's role in my early life? Why did I choose to end my account where I did, papering over our years in the United States? Should I not have written with greater discretion or, contrarily, with greater forthrightness about our identity as Jews? As I was growing up, she more than once would scoldingly urge me to be more modest and more concerned about others' feelings. "Put yourself in his (or her) position," she would repeat. "Don't show off. Don't take credit for what happens to you. Your successes are only half due to you. The other half is due to good luck. Remember Soeur Hélène and Mme. Kalkou. They helped you when you needed it. Now is your turn to help those who are in need. Remember that!" Did I follow her advice as I was writing this book?

Our conversation might continue with questions that touched some raw nerves. I know that, for starters, I would want to ask my mother a simple question: Did your animus toward your brother's Christian lover/wife color your attitudes toward all Christians/Greeks, and did you impute to them all, as a group, the terrible burden of responsibility for what happened to our family following March 1943? You often expressed your gratitude to all those individual Christians/Greeks without whose help we would not have made it. But you think of them as individual people, whereas, for you, the terms *griegos* is all inclusive and is colored by a collective responsibility. Can this be right? Should we not all of us acknowledge the existence of lines that separated us from Greek Christians that sometimes were firm and harsh, while other times these lines were almost imperceptible and flexible? I wish I had the chance to talk with both my parents about these matters and many more.

But time has done its work. Had my mother been alive today, she would have been 106, my father 122. By the time I should have reached my 122nd birthday, perhaps my great-granddaughter (who was born on 6 February of this year, days after I finished the first draft of this book), her mother, and her mother's mother, as well as my other daughter may look at these pages with a smidgen of ironic detachment and ponder if their long-departed ancestor wrote with due modesty and adequate detachment about his Jewish childhood in German-occupied Greece. Perhaps I owe these descendants an explanation. If they come out of reading this small book somewhat befuddled, wondering if there is a sort of ultimate, metaphysical meaning to my and my immediate family's adventures, I would want to reassure them. I am just as puzzled and uncertain about the ultimate meaning of what happened to me during the years of Greece's occupation by the Germans. All these events, dramatic, painful, improbable, disorienting, even ironic as they may appear in retrospect, just happened. There is no inherent logic in them. To be sure, at the root of everything were the evil and brutal actions of a large number of people. But within this context there was a possibility of beating the odds, of being sufficiently lucky to ensure one's survival even in the face of the most determined murder syndicate in the recent history of Europe.

Of the questions my parents might have confronted me with if they had read this book, there is only one I want to try to answer here: What kind of Jews were we? I would have ventured to remind them that we were not terribly religious, although, mostly in memory of our family members and friends who were murdered in Auschwitz, we invariably attended and were genuinely moved during Yom Kippur services in the Monastiriotòn Synagogue at the beginning of every autumn. My grandmother and mother fasted on Yom Kippur, although never my father or any of his brothers. Alongside other Jewish shopkeepers, my father closed his store on Yom Kippur; the metal blinds he drew on that holiday, and kept down for at least twenty-four hours, were at once a sign that usual business was suspended on that day, but also marked the shopkeeper's Jewishness, and therefore his apartness from neighboring Christian shopkeepers. In light of our later experience in the United States, it is significant that not only did we not keep kosher, but in my case, I did not even discover what this ancient ritual meant until my arrival in Cleveland!

Even if, undeniably, we nurtured a general if inchoate sympathy for the State of Israel, which my parents and uncles did not hesitate to express at home or in public, we could not claim to have been convinced Zionists, as this concept had been transmuted into a political ideology in the late nineteenth and twentieth centuries. To this day, I recall with great nostalgia the wonderfully cheerful *Pesach* dinners, when all the family, uncles and aunts and cousins and an occasional stray friend, were gathered around the dinner table at my grandmother's house, my grandmother and father and to a lesser extent Uncle Isaac being the only three in attendance able to read—but only haltingly and not without stumbling along—the ceremonial prayers in Hebrew. We would end up the ritual part of the dinner by singing in Ladino the traditional and playful song, *el cavretico*, and loudly intoning, more or less in unison, *Next Year in Jerusalem*. But none of us had a clear understanding of what that augury signified. In fact, I don't think any one of us thought that such an augury expressed a commitment to the State of Israel and to its policies to its Arab neighbors, none of us, in short, could imagine ourselves as being labeled Zionists as the term has come to be defined in the past few generations. Nor did any one of us seriously consider heeding the Zionist cause to settle in Israel. Strangely, I have a vivid memory of my prewar Armenian nanny, Esther, heeding Stalin's call to return to Armenia, notwithstanding my father's pleading that she should stay put where she was in Greece. Sometime between late 1945 and early 1947, my parents and I walked Esther to the port, where a big steamer was waiting to pick up Armenians who were determined to leave for the promise of a better life in a place that almost no one among them had visited before! We embraced and kissed Esther as she went on board, and never saw her again. A few years later, I recall my father saying that he had received an urgent plea from Esther to help her get back to Salonica. By then, it was impossible to get the Soviet authorities to issue an exit visa to someone such as Esther. I don't recall any comparable departures of relatives or close friends for Palestine or, after 1948, for the State of Israel. Not even in the years immediately following our return to Evzonon Street—a time of great uncertainty and when survivors of the Shoah were in need of guidance and assistance—were we especially attached to the Jewish community's directions. Lukewarm in our religious commitment, rather distant from notions of militant Zionism, and at arm's length from the city's organized Jewish community, still, we were Jews. The experience and the memory of the Shoah left no doubt about that. I would have wished to engage my parents about this position. Obviously, this is a wish that cannot be realized.

But as I close this book, I have a rather different wish: that my two daughters, my granddaughter, and great-granddaughter live long and healthy lives without having to face the sort of challenges my parents and I had to overcome during the terrible years of the Shoah, and its legacy in our lives for decades after the end of World War II.

Postscript

Megaron Presentation

I have heard it said that books are like children: you conceive, nurture and care for them as they grow up (in your house or in your imagination) and then, at a certain point, whether you are ready for it or not, off they go on their own and struggle to establish their own presence in the world. I do think of this book very much in these terms, as a child of mine that will carve its own life, and will stand (or not stand) on its feet, depending on its ability to elicit the interest and benevolence of its readers. The Greek edition already appeared about a year ago, and an incident in the book's brief existence may be worth recounting here, as the English-language edition is about to go to press.

On 13 March of this year (2023) the book was officially presented to the Greek public in the imposing Megaron (the beautiful Music Hall in Athens) before a large number of people, among whom was the President of the Greek Republic. In addition to the president, two small groups of people stood out in the audience: two Catholic nuns dressed in their official garb and a cluster of four or five others, laymen, who surrounded an elderly gentleman who sat through the ceremony deeply absorbed by the proceedings. It turns out that the nuns were members of the Pammakaristos Convent, whose Mother Superior, Soeur Hélène, had been instrumental in saving my family during the war. They had found out about the presentation and wished, by their attendance, to mark the continuity of their convent's mission, from the days when it was flourishing, to the present when no more than a handful of elderly women are members of their Order. My story was for them an integral part of their institution's much larger story. Obviously, they wished that evening to underscore the complex and often challenging responsibilities their Order had discharged through the years. Our meeting afterward was deeply emotional, as we hugged and tried to urge each other to meet again soon—I blurting out words of thanks, they asking me questions about my memories of life in the Convent and pressing me to tell them when I would visit the Convent to have lunch with them.

But it was the elderly gentleman who, at a certain point in the ceremony, literally stole the show, hundreds of pairs of eyes glued to him as he spoke with great eloquence and passion. It turns out that he was Panayotis Kalkou, the widow Kalkou's eldest son, whose family had taken me in and sheltered me in December 1943. Panayotis was now ninety-one years old, and he began to speak with a strong if at moments tremulous voice, recalling his family's war experiences and referring to me as his kid cousin. He described, with an eyewitness's immediacy and vividness, the events I describe in my own book. He spoke of the unknown Jewish kid's arrival at the house, of the intense cold that winter, yet of the warmth that prevailed in the Kalkou household, of the hunger and patience shown by all the children, as time slowly passed and we arrived to the Christmas Eve of that fateful year, and of other folks, especially an Italian soldier who had deserted his unit, who were protected by his mother. He then read a poem that he composed in the 1950s or

1960s, in which he evoked the events and the spirit of Christmas 1943. The crowd listened, spellbound, a sort of religious silence having enveloped the assembled audience. But as he sat down, spontaneously the crowd burst into a loud applause, unclear if it was in memory of his heroic mother or in appreciation of this old man's courage and willingness to take the stage before such a large audience. Suffice it to say that, at the end of the ceremony, as we hugged again and again, we cried openly at such an unexpected encounter, each of us promising the other that this meeting would help reestablish a personal bond that had been interrupted many decades ago; that, in short, two old men could bridge over the time that had elapsed since their previous meeting when they were little boys and now, starting in spring of 2023, allow their memories to bring them close to each other again. I should add that, when Panayotis finished his impassioned intervention, I decided to interrupt the proceedings, so as not to sully the deeply personal tone of his comments. I thought that there would be ample time for presentations. But the experience at the Megaron that evening was altogether special, and it was important, it seemed, to let the moment be remembered as it had happened.

Later, as I was thinking about this unusual (not to say extraordinary) encounter made possible by the reading of this book, I could not help but think back on Pierre Bourdieu's reflections that I mentioned back in the first chapter. Would my very human encounter with Panayotis have been possible if both of us did not have a very clear awareness of the chronology that governed our lives, and of the need to reconstruct our very distant pasts on the basis of these chronologies? Thus, it turns out that this book transformed its presentation from an ordinary, bookish discussion among readers or would-be readers to an intensely emotional experience for everyone present in the Megaron. The book, it seemed to me, had passed its first real test—in that place and time, and before that audience it had managed to establish its presence in the world.

Acknowledgments

Last but by no means least, my thanks to several people who often peeked over my shoulder as I wrote this book, read a page or two as I was struggling with some specific point, or whole chapters, and who, all the while sensitive to the deeply personal nature of my recollections, tried forthrightly to provide me with their critical feedback. Olga Katsiardi was my first fan in this enterprise, and I am very grateful for her ability to transmit to me her enthusiasm, and her insistence that I continue writing. For reasons that explain in the text, I wrote this book in English, but it was first published in Greek. Paris Chronakis, whom I thank warmly, contributed authoritatively and brilliantly to the book's final form—not only to its translation in Greek. Jim Patterson, a great friend from my Brown University days, read every page of the text and enjoined me from abandoning it in the bowels of my computer, as I was tempted to do more than once. Carlo Ginzburg took time from his busy schedule to read the manuscript and urged me to publish it soon and without major changes. I also thank warmly Elsa Amanatidou (of Providence, Rhode Island) and Platon Mavromoustakos (of Athens) for their encouragement and willingness to help. Two English friends, David Ricks and the late Peter Mackridge, experts *sans pareil* in the history and literature of modern Greece, brought their keen stylistic sensitivities to their reading of my memoir and suggested changes that considerably improved my presentation. Two of my beloved "kid" cousins, Flora Molho, uncle Isaac and aunt Rita's daughter, and Tilda Molho, uncle Roufa and aunt Henrietta's daughter, generously shared with me photographs of our childhood years, and did not hesitate, always in good humor, to indicate that on some points in my presentation, their memories did not coincide with mine. I also want to thank, warmly, Wendy Strothman for her interest in the book; her suggestions for improving its organization were very useful. Mr. Izo Avram of Paris generously shared with me a video film of a conversation that took place in his parents' home in Salonica in 1993, in which my mother was present. Mr. Jecky Benmayor of Salonica expertly transcribed and translated my parents' marriage contract, written in solitreo. I am most grateful to him for generously sharing his expertise. Katy Fleming read the entire manuscript and brought her usual enthusiasm and perceptive eye to our discussion of the text. Several other friends, whom I do not wish to embarrass by naming them individually, graciously read bits or chunks of the text and offered their advice. I am grateful to Laura de Angelis, a colleague from the old days at the Faculty of Letters in the University of Florence, for producing the photographs included in the book. My daughter Lilla and her husband Adam Burton, as well as my granddaughter Giulia and her companion Nigel Ward were always ready to provide tactical support, cheerfully assisted by Stella Ward, my ever eager and ingenious great-granddaughter. Not least, my youngest daughter Maria Eirini never failed to remind me that one can always do better. Her advice, that echoed words my mother often addressed to me, has been precious. Zeta Gotsi, my demanding, in-house critic, offered her very keen insights and excellent linguistic help, and not only.

COURAGE AND COMPASSION

My heartfelt thanks to Anna Pataki and to Kostas Kostis, who, from the start, when other publishers in the UK and the United States, were indifferent to the possibility of publishing this book, showed their confidence in it and encouraged me to submit it for publication as soon as I had finished writing it. Marion Berghahn and her very able staff at Berghahn Books—Mark Stanton, Sulaiman Ahmad, and Keara Hagerty—offered excellent suggestions and provided always very useful assistance during the months it took for the book to wind its way through production.

More than once in the following chapters, I refer to an imaginary *cordon sanitaire* that protected me and my parents from the numerous traps we had to avoid during the war. I am convinced that the friends whose names I mention above and the others whom I did not single out by name, formed themselves another sort of improvised shield that protected me as I fumbled my way through the difficult terrain of remembering and recording my memories of a long past and very tumultuous period of time. To members of both these protective shields—the one of nearly eighty years ago, the second of the past few months—I am more indebted than I could express in words.

Before closing, I can't help but recall two people who traveled alongside me a good part of my journey in the years following the war, but whose much too premature deaths, within weeks of each other, puzzle me as much perhaps as does my own survival during the war: my daughter Lisa (who died in March 2016) and my sister Marcella (who died a little earlier, in January 2016). Often, I wonder how they, passionate readers that they were, would have reacted to this memoir and what jokes, corrections, and family stories they would have shared with me if they had been given the gift of a longer life.

In the end, my greatest debt is to my parents, my father, Saul son of Lazar Molho and of Flora Hasson, and my mother, Lily, daughter of Nissim Alkalay and Henrietta Alkalay, and, of course, to my grandmother Flora. Their luminous presence continues to enrich—indeed, to define—my life.

www.ingramcontent.com/pod-product-compliance
Lightning Source LLC
Chambersburg PA
CBHW071338080526
44587CB00017B/2883